Weird, Wacky and Wild

ILLINOIS TRIVIA

David Hudnall & Lisa Wojna

BLUE
BIKE
BOOKS

The Publisher: Blue Bike Books
www.bluebikebooks.com

Library and Archives Canada Cataloguing in Publication

Hudnall, David, 1982–
   Illinois trivia : weird, wacky and wild / David Hudnall and Lisa Wojna.

ISBN 978-1-897278-41-3

   1. Illinois—Miscellanea. I. Wojna, Lisa, 1962– II. Title.
F541.6.H83 2007   977.3   C2007-906368-3

Project Director: Nicholle Carrière
Project Editor: Kathy van Denderen
Production: Vicky Trickett
Illustrations: Peter Tyler, Roger Garcia, Patrick Hénaff and Pat Bidwell
Cover Image: Courtesy of Getty Images; photo by Medioimages/Photodisc

We acknowledge the financial support of the Alberta Foundation for the
Arts for our publishing program.

PC: P5

ACKNOWLEDGMENTS

For their love and support, I want to thank Mom and Dad, Anne and Kathleen, and Jill.

–David

Many thanks to our clever editor, who pieced together the work of two authors and did so seamlessly; to my co-author, David; and to my family—my husband Garry, sons Peter, Matthew and Nathan, daughter Melissa, and granddaughter Jada. Without you, all this and anything else I do in my life would be meaningless.

–Lisa

CONTENTS

INTRODUCTION

Along with nearly three million other people, I currently reside in the city of Chicago. I'm not going to go into why I think it's a great town—if I've done my job, this book ought to take care of that—but I will say, without a shred of embarrassment, that I've lived in the Midwest my entire life, and I like it here. And it's not because I've never been anywhere else; many times I have ventured out of the heart of America and into its arms and legs. And though I've certainly enjoyed the time I've spent on the coasts, in the mountains and down south, the Midwest just feels more *right* to me than any other region of the U.S. And Illinois, the most middle of the Midwestern states, is the star that shines brighter than the others.

I've traveled through Illinois on planes, trains and automobiles (and soon, if all goes according to plan, on a bike), and the state continues to intrigue me in unsuspected ways. So much of the U.S. has become homogenized; every small town now has the same four fast-food restaurants on the same main road. It can get depressing. But there are still towns that haven't been touched by the forces of corporate culture (or at least haven't been dominated by them), and finding these places is one of the most rewarding experiences left in American life. Illinois has these kinds of towns, this authenticity. Tractor pulls, ice cream socials, fireworks, life on the banks of the Mississippi River. America. It really does still exist. You just have to search for it.

I haven't been brainwashed. I'm aware that the land is flat and boring, and I know that the climate is, well, pretty "unsexy." Fields and fields of corn and soybeans are not as scenic as mountains or beaches, but I don't care. I like a challenge, and Illinois, like all worthwhile pursuits, is challenging at times—ask anybody who's endured a Chicago winter. (It really is as miserable as they say it is.) The occasional hardships of Midwestern life are what make us—I'll say it—down-to-earth folks. I wouldn't trade that for anything. I may leave Illinois, but I'll always have the sturdy roots of the Midwest to fall back on (and frankly, I doubt I'll ever get past my suspicions of the East Coast).

In researching this book, I got inspired about Illinois. I made lists of places I hadn't been and wanted to visit, and I found myself delving into topics I knew wouldn't fit into the book—I did it just naturally out of curiosity. The process was interesting to me, and fun. (Meeting the deadline wasn't much fun as a result, but I digress.) So maybe that's the goal of the book: that readers will be inspired to visit some of the places we talk about, or to learn more about the people and history of the state. I definitely will be.

WHAT SETS ILLINOIS APART

In April 2007, in the middle of an otherwise normal spring afternoon, a coyote wandered into a sandwich shop in bustling downtown Chicago. The animal peacefully walked toward the soda cooler, where it rested its tired bones after what had presumably been quite a long trek. Animal Control was quickly called to the scene, and the coyote was taken away and released back into the wild.

In some ways—and maybe this is a stretch, but just go with it—this story is a kind of metaphor for what makes the state of Illinois such a special place. Because no matter how urban Chicago is—and as the third-largest city in the U.S., it certainly qualifies as urban—occurrences such as this will invariably happen to remind you that you're in the middle of the country and that the great outdoors really isn't so far away.

These kinds of dichotomies define Illinois as a state. The downstate farmers and the Chicago bankers. Cripplingly cold winters and heatstroke summers. The Bible Belt and Boystown. Lake Michigan (the fifth-largest lake in the world) and some of the driest prairie lands you're likely to see. They are all Illinois' natural way of "keeping it real"—every extreme is offset by its exact opposite. This is what sets the state apart. It thrives on the push and pull, the friction within its borders. Other states have this to a degree, but not to the extent that Illinois does. Not even close.

It's impossible to talk about Illinois without acknowledging the importance of Chicago—and there's certainly no shortage of information about the Windy City in this book—but it's important to remember that Illinois does not simply exist because Chicago needed a state to call home. There are other cities in the state, believe it or not, full of interesting people, events and history. And if you give them a chance, even some of the smallest towns and counties have their own unique stories to tell. Don't fear the unknown. Turn the page. Welcome to Illinois!

OFFICIAL AND UNOFFICIAL HANDLES

The Name Game

There are several conflicting theories of how Illinois got its name. One story, thought to be erroneous, connects the name to the Illiniwek people, one of a group of six American Native tribes making up the Algonquian nation. In this explanation, *illini* has been translated several ways: "tribe of superior men," "superior men" and "men."

Another, more generally agreed upon explanation points to the origin of the name as coming from the Miami (another Algonquian tribe) word *ilenweewa*, meaning "she/he speaks normally." Both versions of the naming of the state agree that "Illinois" is a French form of the root *illini* or *ilen*. Yet another source explains the state was named after the Illinois River (which got its name from an Illinois Native tribe), and that "Illinois" is the French rendition of the Peoria Native word *iliniwok*. Take your pick.

State Motto

"State Sovereignty, National Union," Illinois' state motto, bold and strong, was adopted in 1819.

In His Memory

Abraham Lincoln's skills as a politician, his dedication to democracy and his humanity are just a few reasons why Illinois salutes him with its official state slogan, "Land of Lincoln." Lincoln moved to Illinois at the age of 21, served his state from 1847 to 1849 in the U.S. House of Representatives and was a member of the Illinois Legislature for four terms, from 1834 to 1841. His family home in Springfield has been named a National Historic Site—and if you're in the area, it's well worth a visit! The Illinois state slogan was officially adopted in 1955.

Holy Aliases Batman!

Were it wanting to hide, Illinois would have enough aliases to choose from. I uncovered no less than six nicknames for Illinois—and there could be more!

☛ Although "Land of Lincoln" is the state's official slogan, it's also bandied about as another Illinois nickname.

☛ Illinois picked up the nickname "The Prairie State" as early as 1842. The name is a salute to the prairie grasses that once covered the state. Illinois is so proud of its prairie grassland that the third week of September is designated "Illinois Prairie Week."

☛ Another longtime favored state nickname is "Garden of the West." Although an exact date on when folks started calling Illinois by this lovely moniker isn't clear, it's apparently been around for some time.

☛ Over the years, corn crops have played a vital role in the state's agriculture, and so it's been aptly touted as "The Corn State."

☛ Being nicknamed "The Sucker State" is probably not such a good thing, but that name too has been around since the early 1800s. Depending on the scholarly source, the name is said to refer to several things: the sucker fish; the suckers who work in the mines (who might make some money but come out aged and weathered); and the poor folk living in the southern portion of the state. Whichever one it is, I'm just glad no one's pinned that nickname on me.

☛ The lush, productive soil of the southern part of Illinois is believed to be the reason for another of Illinois' nicknames, "Egypt," referring to the fertile soils of that country.

And More Nicknames

What do you call someone from Illinois? You have several choices here, too: Illinoisians, Illinoisans or Illinoians. I dare you to try to say that fast.

But hold on a second. There are additional choices too (of course). Other nicknames for folks from Illinois are "Sand-hillers," "Egyptians" and, sadly, "Suckers."

The Great Seal

The first official seal of the Illinois Territory was adopted in 1809. Illinois was the 21st state admitted to the Union on December 3, 1818. The following year, on February 19, the First General Assembly declared it prudent for the new state to have its own Great Seal. It did so, actually adopting the Great Seal of the United States as their own until 1939. At that point, a second Great Seal was adopted. This one was altered slightly, though the eagle mascot of the nation remained front and center. However, the state's motto, "State Sovereignty, National Union," was added.

In January 1867, Sharon Tyndale, secretary of state at that time, decided Illinois needed yet another new Great Seal and encouraged one of the state's senators to bring forth a bill to that effect. The designed was further modified, but not before a little tug-of-war took place between Tyndale and the Senate of the day. Tyndale wanted to use the opportunity of amending the seal to change the wording of the motto, placing the phrase "National Union" before "State Sovereignty." When the Senate discovered his plans, they put the kibosh on them, but Tyndale put his own twist on the seal nonetheless. Although the motto remained the same, the phrase "National Union" is larger and more prominent, and the word "Sovereignty" is spelled backwards. The new seal was officially adopted in 1868, and though it has been re-cut a number of times, it remains true to this third design.

Flying High

The state of Illinois has had two flags flying overhead since entering the Union. The first, adopted on July 6, 1915, was designed by Lucy Derwent in a competition promoted among chapters of the Daughters of the American Revolution. The organization's State Regent Ella Park, who initiated her efforts as early as 1912, spearheaded the idea. The winning design earned its creator $25 and a place in Illinois history. But nothing is ever that simple, is it? Years later, Chief Petty Officer Bruce McDaniel was serving in Vietnam and noticed that the flag of his state was the only one lining the walls of his mess hall that didn't bear the name of its state. In 1969, the General Assembly passed a motion to amend the original flag.

Specifications for a new flag were decided upon, and Mrs. Sanford Hutchison of Greenfield was chosen to design it. This second flag bears the state seal and, of course, the name "Illinois" in block lettering.

Under the Shade

When school children were approached to choose a state tree back in 1907, they voted on the matter. If the vote represented a horse race, it could be said the native oak left its challengers, the maple and elm, in the dust. The native oak emerged as victor with 21,897 votes, maple was a distant second with 16,517 votes, and the lowly elm brought up the rear with 5082 votes. From 1908 to 1973, the native oak was crowned as the state tree, but in 1973 a slight change was made. Another polling of some 900,000 school children that year resulted in a dethroning of the native oak; it was replaced as the state tree by the white oak. With about 20 native species of oak in the state, the white oak garnered the most support from its young electorate with 333,964 votes. The northern red oak was a distant second with 142,247 votes.

Beautiful in Blue

At the same time they were voting on a state tree, school children were called upon to decide another matter—what would be the state flower? Here again the youngsters produced a runaway winner with 16,583 votes cast for the violet. The wild rose came in a respectable second place with 12,628, and golden rod picked up 4315 votes in its third-place finish. Violet was made the official state flower in 1908.

Sing Out Loud

By thy rivers gently flowing, Illinois, Illinois,
O'er thy prairies verdant growing, Illinois, Illinois,
Comes an echo on the breeze.
Rustling through the leafy trees,
And its mellow tones are these, Illinois, Illinois,
And its mellow tones are these, Illinois.

Written by C.H. Chamberlain with music by Archibald Johnston, the song "Illinois" was adopted as the state song at the 54th General Assembly in 1925.

Leader of the Pack

In 1980, maintaining the tradition of conferring with the state's youth, Illinois again asked school children to choose a state animal from the selection of mammals nominated by the General Assembly and Illinois State Museum. Nominees were the raccoon, fox squirrel, opossum, red fox, thirteen-lined ground squirrel and white-tailed deer. The deer emerged the victor, and on January 1, 1982, it became official.

Bird Songs

School children in Illinois were again consulted in 1929 when it came time to choose a state bird. The cardinal won that race with 39,226 votes, the bluebird came in second at 30,306 votes, and the meadowlark, quail and oriole rounded out the top five with 16,237, 15,843 and 15,449 votes, respectively.

Snack Attack!

Whether it's slathered in butter and spiced to your liking or health conscious and plain, Illinois' official snack food is none other than the moviegoer's favorite—popcorn. The popular treat achieved official status in 2003 after Cunningham Elementary schoolteacher Fran Hollister and her class of second and third graders proposed the idea.

State Dance

A heel, toe and a do-si-do— echo these few words in a dance hall anywhere in Illinois and folks will kick up their heels, anxious to take part in their state's official dance. Foursomes have enjoyed the square dance for centuries, but it wasn't officially adopted as the American Folk Dance of the State of Illinois until 1990.

Other Symbols and Emblems

☛ The big bluestem was designated Illinois' official prairie grass on August 31, 1989.

☛ A group of third graders in Dennis School suggested the monarch butterfly, with its signature orange and black colors, should be the state's official insect. It was so named in 1974.

☛ The blue gill was selected as the Illinois state fish and officially so named in 1986. Guess who made the selection? You've got it—the state's school children.

☛ If you guessed school-aged youngsters chose the state reptile, you'd be mistaken. The eastern painted turtle was selected through an Internet vote, and it was made the state's official reptile in July 2005. The eastern box turtle and the common gartersnake were among other contenders for the title.

- An internet vote also decided what the state's official amphibian would be. The eastern tiger salamander took on that honor officially in July 2005. It was up against some pretty stiff competition: the gray treefrog and the American toad.

- Fluorite was named the state's official mineral in 1965. The choice was particularly fitting because Rosiclare and Cave-in-Rock, both in southern Illinois, have the largest deposits of the mineral in the nation.

- Drummer soil, a particularly rich soil ideal for agriculture, was named Illinois' state soil in 2001.

Miniature Monster

In 1958, Mr. Francis Tully discovered the fossil specimen that would later bear his name—the Tully Monster. The animal was soft skinned, lived in the ocean and looked a little like a worm with a fat center and sharp teeth. It was named the state fossil in 1989.

THE WAY THE WIND BLOWS

When it comes to varieties of weather conditions, Illinois has it all—and just about everybody knows it. Located inland, with only the northeastern portion of the state bordering the large body of water that is Lake Michigan, Illinois experiences a largely continental climate. Southern portions of the state are considerably milder than their northern counterpart, and summers can be quite humid, almost subtropical. The state is also well known for its preponderance of stormy conditions in all seasons: winter blizzards, summer tornadoes, heat waves and cold spells.

Law of Averages

If you divide the long, rectangular state of Illinois into three portions, the northernmost portion could expect an average annual temperature of about 50°F, the central portion about 53°F and the southernmost portion about 59°F.

Precipitation Predictions

Similarly, average precipitation levels expected in any given year differ from north to south, with levels generally far higher in the south (48 inches) and lower in the north (36 inches). The north can expect more snow than the south (36 inches versus 10 inches). However, it rains a lot more in the south than it does in the north (46 inches versus 34 inches). Given these facts, the growing season is also vastly different in northern and southern climes, with a length of about 160 days in the north and as many as 210 days in parts of the south.

On average, farmers in Illinois can expect to see rain one of every three days.

Let it Snow, Let it Snow

Chicago wins the prize for recording the largest snowfall in any given year in the state. During the winter of 1978–79, an amazing 90 inches (almost eight feet) of snow fell, challenging road-clearing crews and causing overall chaos. Nature's bounty was blamed for Michael Bilandic, Chicago mayor of the day, losing his seat in the primary election of February 1979. The main reason? Clearing city streets apparently wasn't a priority for his administration, and folks in the Windy City weren't too pleased.

Speaking of Wind...

Apparently Chicago wasn't named the Windy City because of the wind velocity. In fact, the city usually only experiences an average wind speed of 10.4 miles per hour, and there are 16 other U.S. cities far windier and better equipped to earn that title. But exactly how Chicago attracted its Windy City moniker seems to be the subject of at least a couple of legends. One source blames New York journalists in the 1800s who started calling folks in Chicago "the windy citizenry out west" and a few of their leaders "loudmouth and windy." I guess it was the polite way of saying someone was "full of hot air."

However, a story (dated September 22, 1969) in the *Chicago Daily News* says that two patriotic locals came up with the name. According to the article, John Stephan Wright and William Deacon Bross traveled along the east coast bragging about Chicago's many virtues. The "windy" pair were said to have been the impetus for Chicago's other nicknames. In case you were wondering, this Illinois city has several other aliases as well. Here are just a few:

Chicago, Pride of the Rustbelt

Chicagoland

Chi-town

City in a Garden

City of Big Shoulders

Gem of the Prairie

Hog Butcher to the World

"I Will" City

"My Kind of Town"

Packingtown

Second City

"That Toddling Town"

The City That Works

A Storm's Rolling In

If you're into lightning-flashing, thunder-shaking storm watching, Illinois is the place for you. It averages 50 days worth of thunderstorm activity each year.

Highest Temperature

Illinois' all-time hot spot to date is East St. Louis. The city registered a record high of 117°F on July 14, 1954.

Lowest Temperature

The present record for the all-time low in the state goes to Congerville. The mercury dipped to –36°F on January 5, 1999.

Deadly Claim to Fame

Illinois experiences an average of 35 tornadoes a year. The tristate area of Missouri, Illinois and Indiana was also the site of the deadliest tornado in the history of the United States. The killer storm hit on March 18, 1925. The twister started out in Missouri and entered the southwestern portion of Illinois, cutting a wide swath through that state before ending its path of destruction in Indiana. Altogether, the storm traveled 219 miles before losing steam, flattening four towns and damaging six

others along the way. The final tally reported 15,000 homes destroyed, 2000 people injured and another 695 killed. Although all three states suffered the wrath of this storm, Illinois experienced the greatest damage, and of the total deaths, about 600 were Illinoisans. Here are a few other fast facts:

☛ The storm only took 3.5 hours to travel its 219-mile path.

☛ The funnel cloud ranged between one-quarter and one mile in width.

☛ The storm bears the distinction of being the tornado that maintained continuous contact with the ground for the longest time on record.

Weather Stories

So you meet your neighbor—you know, the one you rarely talk to—at the corner market one day. It would be rather rude to pass him by without saying a word, so you dig deep, say hello and shift around for a moment or two in awkward silence. Of course, we all know there's a cure for such a scenario. No matter how many times you've broached the topic that day, a sure remedy for nothing to say is to talk about the weather. In Illinois, climate-related conversation is never dull. The state can hold its own against almost anything Mother Nature has to throw at it. But in case you're short on a weather story of your own, here are a few "remember-when" tidbits from history to keep you going. *(Information retrieved from the National Oceanic and Atmospheric Administration's National Weather Service.)*

January

☛ Tornadoes tend to attack in summer, but on New Year's Day, 1876, an F2-strength tornado actually did some damage in Springfield that winter day.

☛ The first few days of January are typically winter-like in Illinois, but on January 2, 1879, Peoria and Springfield experienced their warmest January nights ever, reporting 59°F and 56°F, respectively.

☛ In the winter of 1884–85, Springfield experienced yet another weather anomaly. The community didn't receive a measurable amount of snowfall until January 5, 1885, setting the record for the "latest first measurable snowfall during a winter season."

☛ On January 12, 1918, Bloomington set a record for an all-time low temperature of –23°F. Although the record was matched on January 20, 1985, it has yet to be broken.

☛ Freezing rain and thunderstorms pelted central Illinois during a three-day period around January 22, 1982. As much as 70 percent of the state was believed to be affected by the glaze from this icing storm.

☛ Southern Illinois was treated to winter's fury on January 16, 1994, with half an inch of ice and accumulations of 6 to 10 inches of snow in some areas.

February

☛ February 19, 1888, was a dark day for folks in Jefferson County. Mother Nature was up to her old tricks again, tossing out the winter chill in favor of one heck of a thunderstorm that resulted in a tornado. About 300 homes and 50 businesses were damaged. And with 80 people injured and 24 dead, the storm is considered the state's ninth deadliest on record.

☛ Folks in Springfield, Decatur and Peoria were likely trading in their winter coats for summer shorts on February 24, 1930. Record high temperatures of 78°F, 75°F and 71°F, respectively, were set in those towns that day.

☛ Spring came early in 1932. On February 10 of that year, Peoria set a record high temperature of 74°F. Springfield (75°), Lincoln (73°), Decatur (71°) and Champaign (68°) also set records for that day.

☛ Central and southern portions of the state experienced whiteout conditions on Valentine's Day 1991. Almost three inches of snow fell, and winds clocked up to 40 miles per hour in some areas. I bet sweethearts opted to stay in that day and find warmer things to do.

☛ Springfield may have recorded near record amounts of snowfall in January 1997, but the next month melted it all away. By February 5, only trace amounts were left, and with little to no snow falling, that February tied the record (previously set in 1935 and tied in 1957 and 1987 respectively) for being Springfield's least snowy.

March

☛ Illinois can expect average temperatures of about 40°F during the month of March, but there's always an exception to every rule. With average temperatures measuring anywhere from 22.6°F in Peoria to 25.6°F in Champaign, 1960 brought the coldest March to date.

☛ On March 8, 1978, Springfield sat under a carpet of snow 16 inches deep—a record for the city.

☛ Talk about paving the state with snow! A winter storm on March 5, 1989, covered a 100-mile wide area of Illinois, from East St. Louis to Danville, with anywhere from 7 to 12 inches of the white stuff.

☛ Tilton's city hall took a beating, along with almost a dozen homes, after a tornado hit that community on March 22, 1991. By the time it made its way to Danville, the storm had charged up about $1 million in damages.

April

☞ On April 2, 1964, the last thing folks in the Windy City likely expected was for their city to be paralyzed by a snow storm. As much as 20 inches of snow fell that day.

☞ Baseball-sized hail pummeled Galesburg on April 5, 1988, causing upwards of $10 million in damages in the process.

☞ The Sears Tower in Chicago took a beating the next day, on April 6, 1988, after strong winds blew out 97 of its windows. The windstorm, clocking between 75 miles per hour in Chicago and 59 miles per hour in Decatur, also toppled the state's oldest tree, a 700-year-old bur oak.

☞ On April 2, 2006, 25 tornadoes (mostly F0s and F1s with winds measuring between 40 and 112 miles per hour) terrorized southeastern and central parts of Illinois.

May

☞ Talk about twisted! A tornado touched down near Neoga in Cumberland County on May 6, 1876, literally blowing a passenger train off its track. All 19 passengers were injured.

☞ The same date more than a century later produced another newsworthy tornado. On May 6, 2003, the southern tip of the state experienced a tornado with wind speeds as high as 210 miles per hour. The storm lasted one hour and 10 minutes and traveled 33 miles, killing two people in its path and injuring another 33.

☞ On May 18, 1883, the north and central parts of Illinois experienced the state's fifth deadliest tornado outbreak to date. Fourteen separate tornadoes touched down, killing 52 people.

☞ Peoria experienced its wettest spring on record in 1927. From March to May an accumulation of 18.64 inches of rain fell.

June

- Pana felt the wrath of Mother Nature when a tornado flattened 25 houses on June 13, 1857.

- Tampico nearly toppled to an F3-strength tornado on June 6, 1874.

- Water was nowhere to be seen in the summer of 1936. In June of that year, Peoria recorded its lowest ever precipitation levels for the month, with less than one inch of rain falling.

- Farmers in the Freeport area fell victim to the tornado of June 22, 1962. A total of 66 barns and 21 homes were destroyed, and two Illinoisans lost their lives.

July

- Peoria, Lincoln, Champaign and Decatur experienced their coolest summers on record in July 1911 with temperatures of 46°F, 44°F, 47°F and 48°F, respectively.

- On July 4, 1980, folks in Springfield were likely praying for a thunderstorm. That day, the National Weather Service reported "11 consecutive hours with a dew point temperature of 80° or higher" before a nice, cool rain finally fell.

☛ A few record high temperatures were set on July 11, 1995, among them being Lincoln at 109°F and Peoria at 108°F.

☛ An astonishing 583 people in Chicago died as a direct result of a heat wave over a four-day period in mid-July 1995. Temperatures hit 105°F "with heat index values peaking at 125°."

August

☛ August 23, 1939, marked the first of a 37-day period where Springfield hadn't recorded a drop of rain. Now that's dry!

☛ A tornado hitting Warren and Mercer counties on August 17, 1948, may have destroyed three barns and two houses, but that was small potatoes compared to the storm that followed. The subsequent hailstorm tallied up millions of dollars worth of damage.

☛ Champaign experienced a deluge of rain with 5.32 inches falling on August 12, 1993. The event marked a record that stands to this day.

☛ Rain fell at a rate of between three and four inches per hour in some parts of Cook County when a thunderstorm hit on August 2, 2001.

September

☛ Flash floods caused $250,000 in damage on September 11, 1974, washing away five bridges in Clark, Crawford and Lawrence counties.

☛ Normally, folks in Peoria don't have to worry about freezing temperatures until mid-October. But that all changed on September 20, 1991. The day marked the "only time in Peoria's recorded history that a freeze has occurred during astronomical summer."

☛ When the mercury dropped to 32°F on September 23, 1995, Springfield experienced its earliest freeze on record. Hmm…so much for global warming.

October

☛ Springfield set a record on October 29, 1925, when 1.8 inches of snow fell. That's the largest accumulation of snow recorded in the state for a 24-hour period in the month of October.

☛ A temperature of 94°F on October 6, 1963, marked Chicago's warmest October on record.

☛ On October 12, 1987, several record lows were set with Rockford and Springfield both reporting 24°F.

☛ October might signal the onset of cooler temperatures for the most part, but on October 24, 2001, thunderstorms and a subsequent tornado in the central portion of the state caused $500,000 in damage.

November

☛ November 1, 1950, was a fairly balmy day in many locations across central Illinois. Pana (84°F), Springfield and Decatur (83°), Peoria (81°) and Champaign (80°) all reported record high temperatures for that day.

☛ A tornado damaged 175 homes across Bond and Fayette counties on November 9, 1984.

☛ On November 19, 1991, a tornado hit the southern Illinois city of Marion. In the span of just 1.5 miles, an estimated $30 million in damages were tallied.

December

☛ The young'uns didn't have to worry about having a white Christmas in the winter of 1830. It was known as the "Winter of the Deep Snow," and between two and three feet of snow fell in December alone.

☛ The same could not be said for Peoria or Springfield in the winter of 1889. Neither community recorded any snowfall for December of that year, and Peoria was also minus the white stuff in December 1890.

☛ Not one, not two, but 19 separate tornadoes caused between $8 million and $10 million in damages on December 18, 1957. One tornado was rated an F5, while several others were F4. A total of 259 people were injured and 13 killed.

☛ By the end of the year in 1990, Peoria set another weather record with 55.63 inches of precipitation falling that year.

THE LAY OF THE LAND

Situated in what's known by its residents as the "Great Lakes Region" (or the East North Central portion of the Midwest by the U.S. Census Bureau), Illinois is bordered by Wisconsin in the far north, Lake Michigan along a portion of the northeastern tip of the state, Missouri and Iowa along its western portion, Kentucky to the south, and Indiana to the east. Geographically speaking, the state is divided into three main areas: the Central Plains, which includes most of Illinois' prairie land and constitutes about 90 percent of the state; the Shawnee Hills, a relatively small portion covering an area roughly 40 by 70 miles along the southern portion of the Central Plains; and the Gulf Coastal region, which takes in most of the area south of Route 50.

Most Populated

"Chicagoland" (a term first coined by the *Chicago Tribune*) includes the city of Chicago, its suburbs and surrounding area. Most Illinoisans, two out of three, in fact, live in Chicagoland.

Size Matters

With a total area of 57,918 square miles, Illinois is the 25th largest state in the nation by area. It's generally long and narrow, measuring 390 miles from north to south and 210 miles from east to west. Of the total area, roughly four percent (2325 square miles) is covered by water.

High Point

At an elevation of 1234 feet, Charles Mound is the highest point in Illinois.

Middle Ground

Overall, the state's average elevation is 600 feet.

Low Point

Illinois' lowest elevation is the Mississippi River, measuring 279 feet.

DID YOU  KNOW?

Thanks to the Wisconsin Glacier, which passed through Champaign County about 10,000 years ago, the county is topped with about 300 feet of glacial soil.

Center Point

The small, Logan County community of Chestnut is the geographic center of Illinois.

Major Lakes

There are only two major lakes in Illinois. Lake Michigan skirts the northeastern section of the state, and Rend Lake is located in the southern portion, in Franklin County.

Main Rivers

Although there are dozens of rivers in Illinois, the four main ones are the Illinois, Mississippi, Ohio and Wabash rivers.

County Curiosities

Illinois boasts 102 counties. As far as population goes, Cook is the largest with 5,303,683 people (2005 population estimates). McLean, however, claims the largest land area with 1184 square miles. Here are a few more county claims to fame:

☛ According to the 2000 Census, roughly 9.3 percent of the population of Bond County lives below the poverty line.

☛ Daniel Boone may have had the majority of his adventures in what's now Kentucky, but his exploits must have made a significant impression on the founders of Boone County since they chose to name their county after him.

☛ Bureau County is actually named after one of its original settlers, Pierre de Beuro, who established a trading post near Bureau Creek back in 1818.

☛ Deer and duck provide a big draw to Brown County for hunters from across the state. One source suggests as many as 40 hunting lodges are located in this relatively small county, which covers a mere 307 square miles.

☛ Calhoun County, also lovingly referred to as the "Kingdom of Calhoun," is actually located on a peninsula that juts between the Mississippi and Illinois rivers.

☛ With the exception of 1920, 1950 and 1960 (which had population increases of 7.3, 5.5 and 2.8 percent, respectively), all other census years reported a decline in population in Carroll County. The most significant population change occcurred in 1990, which recorded a decline of 10.5 percent.

☛ It was in the heart of Beardtown, Cass County, where in 1858, Abraham Lincoln delivered his famous "a house divided cannot stand" speech.

☛ There are three cities in Christian County—Assumption, Pana and Taylorville, the county seat.

☛ When Clark County was initially formed in 1819, it encompassed about one-third of Illinois' total land area.

☛ Clay County is home to the Flora Appleknocker Festival. The festival, held every September, is hosted by the Flora Academic Foundation and draws together business, industry and civic organizations in a venue where they can share information about their careers with school children.

☛ Men in Clinton County earn considerably more than their female counterparts, according to the 2000 census. Their average income is around $36,035 compared with just $23,506 for women.

☛ Census figures in 2000 indicate that there are more females than males in Coles County, with 27,809 women and a mere 25,387 gents.

☛ Located along the shores of Lake Michigan, Cook County is home to Chicago.

- On March 28, 1999, the 103-year-old Crawford County Courthouse in Robinson caught on fire. Since what remained of the initial structure was deemed salvageable by architects in February 2000, the Crawford County Courthouse Committee has been busy raising funds to pay for the necessary repairs.

- Of the 11,253 people living in Cumberland County, about 98.84 percent are Caucasian.

- The community of DeKalb, in DeKalb County, is home to the circa 1929 Egyptian Theatre, an Egyptian-style Art Deco movie palace.

- DeWitt County's motto is "Centered for Growth."

- Coles County lost a good portion of its land in 1859 when 416 square miles of it was seconded to form Douglas County.

- DuPage County is home to the Community Christian Church of Naperville. The *Church Report* ranked the church as the 13th most influential in the country.

- Parts of Clark, Crawford, Edwards, Madison and St. Clair counties, as well as a portion of Knox, Northwest Territory, were used in the formation of Edgar County.

- Although it once comprised almost half of Illinois, Edwards County is now one of the state's smallest counties. Because it was largely settled before the Land Ordinance of 1785 required counties to establish townships, Edwards County does not have any. Instead, it has what are called "Road Districts."

- Effingham County is on a major transportation route. It's situated at the juncture of Interstate 57 (which links Chicago to the Gulf of Mexico) and Interstate 70 (which connects the east to the west).

☛ Fayette County has the dubious distinction of being home to the Vandalia Correctional Center, an Illinois state prison.

☛ Ford County was the last of the state's 102 counties to be formed. It was made official on February 17, 1859.

☛ Bill Swango, one of the country's most preeminent woodcarvers, makes his home in Fulton County.

☛ The population of Gallatin County is predominantly white. About 98.37 percent of the county declared themselves as such in the 2000 census.

☛ The Kickapoo and Pottawatamie tribes first warred over who had claim to the area Greene County now occupies. The first white explorer to the area was La Salle in 1759.

☛ If its name is any indication, Grundy County must have been praying for a law-abiding future when William E. Armstrong helped form the county. It was named after

Felix Grundy who was considered by many historians as the "greatest criminal lawyer Tennessee ever had."

☛ Most of the 815 square miles forming Hancock County was initially set aside as a place where veterans of the War of 1812 could settle.

☛ Henderson County, Illinois, was named after Henderson County, Virginia, which was named after Richard Henderson. Henderson founded Transylvania Colony in 1775, but the following year Henderson's claim to the land was invalidated, and Transylvania Colony was no more.

☛ Henry County has had four county seats throughout the years: Richmond (1837–39), Geneseo (1839–40), Morristown (1840–43) and Cambridge (1843–present).

☛ Iroquois County was so named, according to legend, after a band of Iroquois were defeated along the Iroquois River. It's the only county in the country with that name.

☛ Human habitation in Jackson County dates back 11,500 years. The county conducts ongoing research into the area's early formation.

☛ Most of the residents of Jasper County, 99.15 percent, are white.

☛ Continental Tire North America, established in Jefferson County back in 1974, is the county's largest employer, boasting 2100 workers.

☞ Jersey County calls itself a "hunter's and fisher's paradise." Among the wild game are quail, deer, squirrel, rabbit and wild turkey.

☞ Looks can be deceiving. Although Jo Daviess County looks like it should have a hard "e" sound, it's actually pronounced as "Davis."

☞ Some folks refer to Johnson County as "The Bicycling Capital of Illinois."

☞ With a population of 404,119 in 2000, Kane County is the fifth most populated county in the state.

☞ Kankakee County is more ethnically diverse than some of Illinois' other counties, with 79.89 percent of its population made up of white Americans, 15.47 percent African American and, to a smaller degree, Native American, Asian, Pacific Islander and other groups.

☞ Although it has an estimated population of only 88,158, in March 2007, Kendall County was cited by the Census Bureau as the "second-fastest growing county in the United States between the years 2000 and 2006."

☞ Knox County was first established in 1825, but it wasn't until 1839 that the county borders were finalized.

☞ With 75 inland lakes and the largest amusement park in the Midwest, it makes sense that Lake County's motto is "Natural Spaces, Fun Places."

☞ LaSalle County claims to be the second-largest county in the state, covering 1148 square miles.

☞ Captain James Lawrence, who died while commanding the USS *Chesapeake,* was honored in the naming of Lawrence County. He is also known for his dying words: "Don't give up the ship."

☞ Lee County was formed in 1839, and its county seat is Dixon.

☞ The fictional town of Haddonfield, featured in the 1978 low-budget horror film *Halloween,* was located in Livingston County. Incidentally, the independent film, which was made on a shoestring budget of just over $300,000, grossed $47 million, making it one of the most successful films of its kind.

☞ As a lawyer, long before his ascent to fame, Abraham Lincoln was a frequent visitor to the Logan County courthouse.

☞ Macon County is named for Honorable Nathaniel Macon of North Carolina in 1829. Macon was so well known and respected a politician throughout the country at the time that three other states named a county after him: North Carolina, Georgia and Alabama. He was also quite a character, ordering that a feast and "grog" be served at his funeral, and that friends toss stones instead of earth on his casket. Macon is buried alongside his wife, son and grandson, and large mounds of stones mark their gravesites.

☞ Where Macoupin County derived its name from seems a bit of a mystery. One theory is that it came from a Native American word meaning "white potato," but linguists don't believe that, since the potato wasn't grown there at the time. Another theory is that the word refers to edible root plants such as the arrowhead or the American lotus. Either way, what we do know is the county was formed from Green and Madison counties in 1829.

☞ Madison County was formed in 1812 and named after the fourth (and then reigning) president of the United States, James Madison. Initially, Madison County was most of the northern portion of the state, but its size was reduced just two years later with the formation of Edwards County.

☞ Marion County was formed in 1823 out of parts of Jefferson, Fayette, Crawford, Edwards, Gallatin, Madison, Randolph, St. Clair and Knox, Northwest Territory.

☞ Census figures in 2006 put the population of Marshall County at 13,003, a decrease from the 2000 figure of 13,180.

☞ A busy post during the French and Indian War of 1757, Fort Massac State Park—located in Massac County—is the oldest state park in Illinois.

☞ McDonough County was established on January 25, 1826, but its organization was not complete until June 14, 1930.

☞ Based on a 2006 population estimate of 315,373, McHenry County is the sixth-largest county in the state.

☞ McLean County leads the state in the production of corn and soybeans.

☞ Monroe County was established in 1816 by carving a portion of the southern part of Randolph and northern section of St. Clair counties and claiming them as its own.

☛ Montgomery County was named in honor of American Revolutionary War general Richard Montgomery. In 1775 he was killed in an attempt to capture Quebec City, Quebec, Canada.

☛ In its 179 years of existence, Morgan County has had three county courthouses. The first was built in 1826 but burned just a year later. The second was erected in 1830 and housed county legal business until 1868 when the current courthouse was completed, which still stands and is operational to this day.

☛ Moultrie County is a small county of 344 square miles with five neighbors: Macon County to the northwest, Piatt County in the north, Douglas and Coles Counties to the east and Shelby County to the south.

☛ Covering 757 square miles, Ogle County is the state's 17th-largest county.

☛ Men in Peoria County fare considerably better than their female counterparts when it comes to annual personal income. Men on average draw a salary of about $40,840, but women only average $25,335 a year.

☛ Coal mining formed the economic backbone of Perry County for its first 100 years. The Du Quoin State Fairgrounds and the Pyramid State Park are reclaimed strip mines turned into recreation areas.

☛ Piatt County covers 440 square miles, 91 percent of which is cropland.

☛ Pike County and Vermilion County have a unique quality in common. Both Illinois counties border a county of the same name in a different state: Pike County, Missouri, and Vermillion County, Indiana.

☛ The first permanent settlement in Pope County was where Golconda now stands. Golconda is also the county seat.

☛ Polish nobility was honored in the naming of Pulaski County. Although he died as a result of injuries incurred from the Revolutionary War in 1779, and the county wasn't formed until 1843, Count Casimir Pulaski was recognized for his abilities as a stellar cavalry officer.

☛ At a scant 166 square miles, Putnam County is Illinois' smallest county.

☛ "Where Illinois Began" is Randolph County's motto.

☛ Rock Island County is home to the Niabi Zoo. Covering more than 40 acres and boasting as many as 900 animals, the zoo certainly lives up to its Osage Native name, which means "young deer spared by the hunter."

☛ Known for his prowess as a warrior and accuracy as a prophet, Shawnee chief Tecumseh is memorialized with a bronze statue located at the Saline County Conservation area in Saline County. It's the only known bronze statue of this brave hero. Saline County also calls itself "Garden of the Gods Country."

☛ The site of the city of Springfield was decided on by the simple action of driving a wooden stake into a field near Spring Creek, Sangamon County. Likely the three commissioners of the day who chose the site as their county seat had no idea it would also serve as the state's capital.

☛ Calvin Hobart and O. Matheny were the first white settlers to put down roots in what is now Schuyler County.

☛ Folks in Illinois are mighty proud to say Abraham Lincoln spent a considerable part of his early life in Illinois. For example, the motto for Scott County is "Walk Where Lincoln Walked." Imagine if he'd been born in the state.

☛ The Shelby County Courthouse, located in Shelbyville, the county seat, took 1,750,000 bricks to build. Moses Flanders, the owner of a brickyard in Shelbyville, was awarded the contract to supply the materials at a cost of "$6.00 per thousand."

☛ Stark County calls itself "Central Illinois' Best Kept Secret!"

☛ Stephenson County prides itself in being the site of "the second Lincoln-Douglas debate, August 27, 1858."

☛ Pekin is Tazewell County's largest city and county seat.

☛ Union County and the state of Illinois have something in common—they both became official in 1818. That's when Union County was formed and the state joined the Union.

☛ Of the 12,938 residents living in Wabash County, according to the 2000 Census, most (7982) live in the county seat, Mount Carmel.

☛ In the Warren County Courthouse, Mormon prophet and founder Joseph Smith faced an extradition hearing in June 1841. The charges of murder, polygamy and other crimes were later dropped.

☛ Census figures in 2000 indicate that men may have more choice in dating than women in Washington County. That's because for every 100 females, there are 97.60 males.

☛ On average, men in Wayne County earn about $29,148 a year, whereas women earn about $20,989, according to the 2000 Census.

☛ Agriculture was the backbone for the economy of White County until the summer of 1939, when it was found that the fields contained more than good earth. Oil was discovered, and the rest, as they say, is history.

☛ When it comes to promoting healthy habits, Whiteside County could be a nation leader. In the spring of 2007, the county held a number of forums promoting the idea of a smoke-free Whiteside County. The initial goal is to encourage a minimum of 300 households to pledge to have smoke-free homes and cars. Way to go!

☛ According to its website, Will County leads the state in population growth and new home construction.

☛ Because Interstates 24 and 57, and Illinois Route 13, intersect in Williamson County, it's no wonder the county considers itself the "Hub for Southern Illinois."

☛ Although it's not the most populous county, when you do the math, Winnebago County's 278,418 residents are nice and snug at about 542 people every square mile.

☛ Abraham Lincoln may not have been born and raised in Illinois, but another president certainly was: Ronald Reagan. A trail has been marked leading visitors through the communities important to Reagan's life, and part of the trail goes right through Woodford County.

MOTHER NATURE VERSUS FATHER TIME

Breeding Ground

It may not have looked like much to the European settlers first arriving on the Illinois prairie, but what was underneath the prairie grass and wildflowers was rich soil that founded a stellar agriculture industry. The region also provides habitat to as many as 297 bird species, 196 fish species and 63 mammal species. Here's a sampling of what you might spot in the state's many natural areas:

☛ The tupelo gum tree can grow to a height of up to 90 feet in swampland or standing water and can live 1000 years. Interestingly, though the tree grows in a wet environment, its seeds must be dry in order for them to germinate.

☛ They're considered one of the state's endangered species, but yellow-headed blackbirds can be glimpsed now and again if you're watchful. With a brilliant yellow head and throat crowning a jet-black body, the bird is recognizable as soon as you see it!

☛ They may have been plentiful in the early days of the state, but today, populations of the big-eared bat, gray bat and Indiana bat are all taking a beating in the mammal category, along with the Rafinesque's, southeastern myotis and eastern woodrat. All are listed on Illinois' endangered species list. The gray/timber wolf, rice rat, golden mouse and eastern squirrel are a little more plentiful, but not by much. They are all on the threatened species list.

☛ The only place you can find the Illinois mud turtle, or yellow mud turtle, is in the northwestern portion of Illinois and in Iowa and Missouri. All three states list this turtle as an endangered species.

Artificial Beauty

With 26,000 acres of water surrounded by 11,000 acres of land, Carlyle Lake is the biggest artificial lake in the state. Here are a few other Carlyle characteristics:

☛ There are more than 30 species of fish in the lake, including bass, bluegill, crappie and walleye.

☛ Producing an estimated 3260 pounds of fish per water acre, the areas below both the Carlyle Dam East Spillway and Carlyle Dam West are considered among the most productive fishing areas in the state.

- The area is also considered one of the best locations in Illinois for hunting waterfowl, as well as white-tailed deer, squirrels and rabbits.

- If you'd rather shoot your prey with a camera, more than 200 species of migratory birds make their home at various times throughout the year in the Carlyle area.

National Pride

The government of Illinois and numerous conservation groups throughout the state take the topic of conserving their natural environment seriously. Illinois is also home to one national wildlife area, the Shawnee National Forest. This pristine wilderness takes up 261,357 acres of the southern tip of the state. Forestry officials boast that the area is home to "at least 48 species of mammals, 237 birds, 52 reptiles, 57 amphibians, 109 fish... (and) 500 vertebrate species." Some of the more exotic creatures hidden away in the area include the Indiana bat, pygmy sunfish, and blind cavefish. The Shawnee National Forest celebrated its 100th anniversary in 2005.

DID YOU KNOW?

Carlyle Lake was the site of the 1994 U.S. Olympic Festival Sailing Competition.

Solid Ground?

If you think living in Illinois makes you safe from potential earthquakes, think again. On average, the state experiences at least one earth-shaking experience each year. Most are just a vibration, but those living in the area still feel it. Some earthquakes, however, have caused minor damage. Here are a few of the more impressive rumblings:

☛ The first recorded earthquake in the state occurred on January 8, 1795, near Fort Kaskaskia.

☛ Folks must have wondered who was playing a trick when on October 31, 1895, an earthquake measuring 6.8 on the Richter scale hit near Charleston, Missouri. The earthquake was felt in 23 states, from Bertrand, Montana, to Cairo, Illinois.

☛ On Tuesday, September 2, 1999, a smaller earthquake hit the northern part of the state near Dixon. It measured 3.5 on the Richter scale, and some folks in the area thought it was a mining blast.

☛ Southeastern Illinois usually experiences some minor damage from an earthquake every 20 years or so. The most recent to hit that area was in June 1987. It measured 5.0 on the Richter scale.

(*Source: Illinois State Geological Survey*)

Underground Activity

Never mind earthquake action, Illinois also has its very own volcano…sort of. Hicks Dome, located in Saline County, is the site of a would-be volcano that experts believe exploded underground 150,000,000 years ago. All you can see, however, is a substantial mound and other unusual formations. Of course, since the theory isn't backed by physical proof, such as a collection of volcanic rock for example, the geological disturbance is actually called a "crypto-explosion."

U.S. CENSUS

One, Two, Three...

The population of Illinois, based on the 2000 U.S. Census, was 12,419,293 (2006 estimates put that number at closer to 12,831,970), making it the fifth most populated state in the country. Spread that number out over the entire state and that's the equivalent of 223.4 persons per square mile.

Breaking It Down

Generally speaking, the population of Illinois looks something like this:

☞ 7 percent are under the age of five.

☞ 25.4 percent are under 18.

☞ 12 percent are 65 or older.

☞ 50.9 percent are female.

☞ 12.3 percent were born in a country other than the U.S.

☞ 19.2 percent of folks aged five years and older speak a language other than English at home.

☞ 81.4 percent aged 25 years and older are high school graduates, bettering the national average by a full percentage point.

☞ 26.1 percent aged 25 years and older have earned a bachelor's degree or higher, again bettering the national average of 24.4 percent.

☞ Of the population aged five and older, 1,999,717 people struggle with some type of disability.

Ethnic Diversity

The following Illinois statistics are based on 2005 estimates from the U.S. Census Bureau.

Race	Percentage of Population*
White (non-Hispanic)	65.8
Black	15.1
Hispanic or Latino	14.3
Asian	4.1
Persons with two or more ethnic backgrounds	1.1
American Indian and Alaska Native	0.3
Native Hawaiian and Other Pacific Islander	0.1

*Note: The "Hispanic or Latino" category can include people of any race, which is why the figures don't add up to 100 percent.

Illinois Population Through the Years

Census Year	Population
1800	2,458
1850	851,470
1860	1,711,951
1870	2,539,891
1880	3,077,871
1890	3,826,352
1900	4,821.550
1950	8,712,176
1980	11,426,518
2000	12,419,293

Population by Ancestry

The five most prominent ethnic backgrounds in Illinois are:

- German at 19.6 percent of the population

- African American at 15.1 percent

- Irish at 12.2 percent

- Mexican at 9.2 percent

- Polish at 7.5 percent

DID YOU  KNOW?

The largest 10-year increase in population, percentage-wise, in Illinois occurred during the early years of the state. Between 1800 and 1810, the population grew from 2458 to 12,282, or 399.7 percent. Between 1900 and 2000, the population almost tripled, increasing from 4.8 million to 12.4 million.

County by County

The seven largest counties in Illinois, based on 2000 population figures, are Cook (5,376,741), DuPage (904,161), Lake (644,356), Will (502,266), Kane (404,119), Winnebago (278,418) and McHenry (260,077).

Behind Closed Doors

Of the total population of Illinois, 321,781 people live in some type of group facility. Here's where:

- ☛ 91,887 live in a nursing home

- ☛ 90,463 live in a college dormitory

- ☛ 67,820 reside in a correctional facility

- ☛ 45,726 live in some other group accommodation

- ☛ 15,020 live in some other type of custodial institution such as schools, hospitals and so on

- ☛ 10,865 live in military quarters

Middle of the Road
The median age of folks in Illinois, according to U.S. Census 2000 figures, is 32.8 years. The largest population for both males and females is in the 35–39 age group.

Golden Years
On average, folks in Illinois can expect to see their 73rd birthday.

According to 2000 Census figures, Chicago is the third most populated city in the U.S. New York comes in first place with 8,008,278 residents and Los Angeles in second with 3,694,820 residents.

Top Ten

Springfield might be the capital of Illinois, but it's running in the middle of the pack when it comes to the state's 10 most populated cities. Here's the breakdown, based on U.S. Census 2000 figures:

City	Population
Chicago	2,896,061
Rockford	150,115
Aurora	142,990
Naperville	128,358
Peoria	112,936
Springfield	111,454
Joliet	106,221
Elgin	94,487
Waukegan	87,901
Cicero	85,616

Home and Work

About 67.3 percent of Illinoisans own their homes. For most of these folks, it takes an average of 28 minutes to travel between their home sweet home and the job that helps pay the bills.

The Name Game

Between 2000 and 2004, Jacob and Michael fought it out over the top two most popular names for boys. Jacob rated first in 2000, 2001 and 2004, but Michael beat him out for first place in 2002 and 2003. Whichever name wasn't in first place landed in second. For girls, Emily was in the top spot from 2000 to 2004. Hannah came in second place in 2000 and 2001, but was replaced by Emma from 2002 to 2004.

ROADSIDE ATTRACTIONS

Gentle Giant

Robert Pershing Waldow was considered a gentle giant by many who knew him. Born in Alton in 1918, he entered the world weighing eight pounds and six ounces—nothing too unusual about that. But by the age of six months, little Bobby's weight had almost quadrupled to 30 pounds, and his growth pattern after that never really slowed. At the time of his death in 1940, at the age of 22, big Bobby had become the tallest man in U.S. history, measuring an astounding 8 feet 11 inches and weighing 490 pounds. During his short lifetime, he was known as an inspirational example of someone overcoming what could have been a devastating handicap and living life to its fullest and inspiring all he met. In his memory, a group of citizens organized the creation of a life-size bronze statue. In 1985 it was erected just off College Avenue at the Southern Illinois University School of Dental Medicine.

Naval Mascot

During World War II, a 700-pound pig brought folks a lot of joy—and no, he wasn't on a spit. Dubbed "King Neptune" by his original owner, a navy recruiter named Don Lingle, the proud porker was toured around the country on an auction-circuit of sorts. Folks continuously bid on the pig at war bond rallies, only to hand him back to his original owner for the next auction. King Neptune died in 1950, and if you're interested in paying your respects, you can view his grave in Mount Pleasant. His tombstone reads: "King Neptune, 1941–1950. Buried here, King Neptune, famous navy mascot pig. Auctioned for $19,000,000 in War Bonds, 1942–1946, to help make a free world."

Peace, Man!

If you ever were, are, or wanted to be a hippie, a drive past the world's only Hippie Memorial is most definitely in order. Located on Arcola's Oak Street, the memorial was the brain-child of self-confessed hippie Bob Moomaw. A colorful character to be sure, Bob believed in freedom of self-expression—his and everyone else's. The metal and wood creation that makes up the memorial is 62 feet long, and even though Moomaw passed away in 1998, it still graces the town's downtown core.

Saluting the Amish

About 220 acres consisting of rock gardens and assorted buildings has attracted visitors to Arcola, often referred to as the "Heart of Amish Country," since 1958. That's when the Rockome Gardens first opened their doors for business. Visitors can tour the lush flower gardens on their way to a haunted cave, the old schoolhouse, blacksmith shop, farmhouse, buggy rides or model trains. Organizers promise a little something for everyone, with special events and displays such as the annual Amish Country Cheese Festival, which highlights the Amish way of life. The attraction is located five miles west of I-57 at Exit 203.

The Spindle

Talk about unique advertising gimmicks! If stores at the Cermak Plaza Shopping Center don't attract shoppers, the roadside attraction certainly will. Eight perfectly good-looking cars are impaled on a 40-foot spike—a modernist sculpture created by Los Angeles artist Dustin Shuler in 1989. "The Spindle," as it came to be named, has become so famous it even had a cameo appearance in the movie *Wayne's World*.

DID YOU KNOW?

With 153 washers, 148 dryers and 15 flat-screen TVs occupying 13,500 square feet of space, Berwyn boasts the world's largest laundromat. And that's not its only claim to fame. The energy required to run the place is supplied by 36 solar panels, each measuring 10 x 4 feet, making the entire operation energy efficient as well.

Howdy Partner!

Union is home to a throwback to the country's earlier days. Donley's Wild West Town has been a tourist destination since 1975. As the name implies, the site offers a replica of what an early-day pioneer town must have looked like. Along with the typical saloon, it has blacksmith shops, pioneer homes, a train and much more. Antique collectibles throughout the village add a touch of authenticity to the mock gunfights or old-fashioned Wild West shows that occur sporadically. And if you're hungry, chow down at the on-site restaurant that, like the rest of the experience, takes you back to them good old days.

Remembering the Victims

Twenty-eight people died in Plainfield on August 28, 1990, after an F5 tornado tore through the community in the mid-afternoon. In their memory, the Tornado Memorial was erected near the town's high school. Inscribed on the black marble, along with the names of each of the victims, is the simple phrase: "The tornado's path of destruction."

Railroad Disaster

Just three miles east of Chatsworth, the nation experienced one of its worst railroad disasters in history. Known as the "Chatsworth Wreck of 1887," a train traveling the Peoria, Toledo and Western Railway line passed over a burning trestle that subsequently collapsed. Of the 500 passengers on board, as many as 372 were injured and 85 killed. A memorial was erected 2.5 miles east of the town.

Giant Graves

On June 22, 1918, a circus train was rear-ended by another train near Forest Park. Between 56 and 61 circus performers were killed. Today, the site of the accident, known as Showmen's Rest, is marked by five full-sized elephant statues with their trunks down to indicate they are in mourning.

At least two elephants are buried in Illinois. Carson and Barnes Circus elephant Kay is buried in Taylorville, her grave marked with a modest headstone; and a monument to Clark and Walters Circus star Norma Jean graces her graveside in Oquawka.

Sports Salute

In the middle of Chicago's Michigan Avenue is a monument to Cubs announcer Jack Brickhouse. Situated on a sidewalk is a cube-shaped announcer's desk with a likeness of Brickhouse from the waist up speaking into a microphone.

Tut, Tut!

King Tut is buried in Carbondale. Well, sort of. King Tut was the name of a saluki, an Egyptian breed of hunting dog, which was purchased as a school mascot for Southern Illinois University's sports teams. The mascot was chosen because the area where the university is located is nicknamed "Little Egypt." Sadly, the mutt found himself under the wheels of a car in 1954 and was buried in a corner of the school's McAndrew Stadium. Although Astroturf covers his grave, officials erected a small pyramid at the site to honor the pooch.

Entertainment Bank

Talk about taking the pain away from long bank line-ups. The Union Federal Savings and Loan in Kewanee has taken great pains to give their customers something to look forward to while waiting. It seems the bank installed a climate-controlled play pool for two Nearctic American river otters.

Condo Heaven

Home to less than 1300 people, Griggsville calls itself the "Purple Martin Capital of the Nation." To be truthful, the claim didn't come about as a result of Mother Nature choosing Griggsville for its purple-winged wonders. Instead, it was through an effort to rid the town of mosquitoes without using chemical pesticides back in the 1960s. That's when a local antenna manufacturer named J.L. Wade discovered the town was situated in the purple martin's migratory path. Because one purple martin can consume as many as 2000 mosquitoes per day, all Griggsville had to do was provide these feathered friends with a reason to stay. That's when Wade decided to build a 562-room high-rise apartment building that stretched 70 feet into the sky. The finished birdhouse was erected in 1962.

Look Up!

Maybe it's because it's located in the Land of Lincoln, but the fiberglass, ax-wielding giant Paul Bunyan statue situated beside Bessie the Cow and a super-sized milk bottle on Lamb's Farm on Rockland Road in Libertyville looks a lot like Abe himself. Check it out!

Sweet Memorial

If you're passing by the Lincoln passenger depot, you're likely to notice a rather unique monument. Perched on a mount is a replica of a large watermelon quarter. As with any other monument, the story that goes along with it answers all the obvious questions. Railroad tracks were first laid through Logan County in 1853. When developers decided on the perfect site for a town, they named it, after Abraham Lincoln, who was a lawyer representing the railroad at the time. Lincoln himself christened the newly laid tracks during a formal ceremony held on August 27, 1853. After sorting through a wagon full of watermelons, he purchased one from a local farmer and doled out slices to folks in attendance. Then he cut into one and used its juice to christen the railroad tracks.

Fairground Lincoln

Carl W. Rinnus of Springfield immortalized Abraham Lincoln's clean-shaven side. The 30-foot-tall fiberglass structure shows a young, lean and whiskerless Lincoln holding an ax. The statue was erected near the entry to the Illinois State Fair Grounds in Springfield in time for the 1967 fair.

The Sailor Man

If you don't know the story behind it, the six-foot bronze statue of the comic character Popeye the Sailor Man proudly perched in Segar Memorial Park may seem a bit odd. But a quick read of the accompanying plaque bearing his name clears up any confusion. The statue was erected in 1977 as a salute to Elzie Segar, Popeye's creator. He was born in Chester in 1894.

Condiment Crazy

Who said there was no other kind than Heinz? Folks in Collinsville have known for a long time now that Brooks Catsup is best! In a salute to the product, a 170-foot-tall water tower shaped in the form of a bottle of Brooks Catsup was erected in 1949 near Route 159. In 1995, after more than 50 years of being bruised and battered by the elements, the roadside wonder, dubbed the "World's Largest Catsup Bottle," was nearly tossed into the landfill until the Catsup Bottle Preservation Group got involved and raised the funds needed for repairs. The landmark was entered into the National Register of Historic Places in August 2002.

Golden Arches

If you're passing through Des Plaines' Lee Street during the summer months and find yourself passing by a McDonald's restaurant advertising burgers for 15 cents, don't get too excited. Chances are you've come upon McDonald's USA First Store Museum, an exact replica of the first McDonald's restaurant opened in the city by franchise founder Ray Kroc. It's located on the site of the original store, which was torn down in 1984. The rebuild followed the original blueprints, and the restaurant's interior is all original, right down to the barrel that the all-male staff would have drawn the root beer from. And just in case reading this has you craving a Big Mac, don't fret. There's a fully operational McDonald's right across the street.

Man's Best Friend

Good Ole Boomer didn't stand a chance the day he died. The story goes that the three-legged wonder dog was trying to save his master when he was killed on a railroad bridge in 1859. A monument to the canine hero can be seen in downtown Makanda.

Wait. Where am I?

Shake your head all you want; you're not seeing things. That 94-foot-tall building that is leaning a little too much to one side appears a lot like its inspiration in Italy. The Leaning Tower of Niles is a half-sized replica of the Leaning Tower of Pisa. It was just one part of a park constructed by Robert Ilg in 1932.

The Leaning Tower replica was built to cover the water tank of the park's pool. The Ilg family officially dedicated the unique attraction to the village in 1996. It was restored in 1997. Interestingly, the Italian city of Pisa is one of Niles' four sister cities. They entered into that sisterhood in 1991.

A Sign from God

When worshippers at The First Baptist Church of Effingham were deciding on a way to reach out to folks who never grace a church doorstep, they came upon the idea of erecting a giant cross. Standing 198 feet tall, the finished product is situated at the intersection of Interstates 57 and 70. The church estimates that about 50,000 travelers pass the site daily, and they hope the cross is an inspiration to them all.

OUT OF THIS WORLD

Halloween All Year Long

You'd best gather all your courage before making your way to Burbank's Haunted Trails Amusement Park, which has some of the scariest haunted house scenes ever. Along with a 600-foot "maze of sheer terror," the area boasts the best in amusement park activities, including a miniature golf course that comes with four miniature haunted houses of its own.

Peaceful Paradise

If a visit to the Anderson Japanese Garden website is any indication of the peacefulness of the area, most of us should book ourselves a visit. The goal of organizers was to produce "one of the most authentic Japanese gardens in the world…[and] open minds to a different culture while offering guests a place of peace and tranquility where they will find healing, renewal, inspiration, and a re-energized soul."

The idea to develop the area in this way was initially the brainchild of John Anderson in 1966. John and his wife Linda had purchased land in Rockford to build a home, and they believed the area was also suited to a Japanese garden—something they'd acquired an appreciation for during their visits to Japan. The entire site was designed by Hoichi Kurisu and is divided into two gardens: one reflecting the Kamakura period from 1185 to 1333 AD, and a second area, including a teahouse and other amenities, reflective of 16th-century Sukiya style. In 1998 the Andersons donated their garden to an independent, not-for-profit charity.

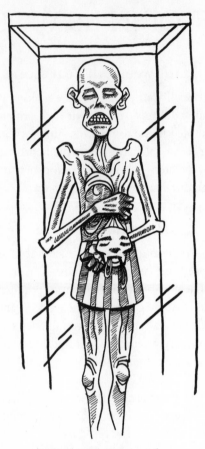

Medical Marvels

Tucked away in the corner of the Southern Illinois University School of Medicine in Springfield is a tribute to the history of health care in the form of a rather unique collection of artifacts and heritage items on display in the Pearson Museum. Officially dedicated in 1980, the museum's curator guides visitors through the museum, sharing the history of the artifacts on display and explaining age-old medical practices, such as the use of leeches in bloodletting. But be sure you have a tough stomach before tackling this historic site. Rumor has it that along with a complete skeleton, the museum houses many human body parts.

Golf Anyone?

Talk about unwinding a little after a tough day at the office. For the folks operating the Ahlgrims Funeral Parlor in Palatine, taking your mind off the job is as simple as a trip to the basement, where, along with a ping-pong table, a shuffleboard table and video games, there's a complete nine-hole miniature golf course. To successfully maneuver through the course, you'll have to pass an upright coffin, haunted house and other ghoulish obstacles. Apparently local groups have been known to hold their meetings in the basement, and the facilities are open—free of charge—to the general public. But you should call ahead to make sure a funeral isn't in progress.

Way Out There

The Lakeview Museum of Arts and Sciences in Peoria offers a lot more than a dusty collection of artifacts. According to its website, the museum offers the "world's largest scale model of the solar system," and to prove it, it's been in the *Guinness Book of Records* since 1992. (A museum in Maine has attempted to trump Lakeview's claim by erecting what they believe is a larger exhibit, but the jury's still out on that.) The museum also has a planetarium and dedicates space to permanent and traveling exhibits.

Tribute to the Pharaohs

When Jim and Linda Onan of Wadsworth heard theories about pyramids attracting mysterious and magical powers, they decided to build their house in the shape of one. The end result is a 17,000-square-foot, six-story, 24-karat gold-plated building they call home. Considered a piece of art in its own right, the building is protected by a 64-foot-tall statue of King Ramses, and the Onans' three cars are kept in three identical, side-by-side pyramids of their own! The family used to conduct tours of their house but hasn't done so for a while. Still, it's an amazing sight from the road, and you can catch glimpses of it online by googling "gold pyramid house."

Fine Lines

Located in Quincy, the Gardner Museum of Architecture and Design is hard to miss. Housed in the old Quincy Public Library, the limestone structure is Romanesque Revival in style, was erected in 1888, and speaks to the mission of the museum: "to foster an increased awareness and appreciation of the architectural and design heritage of Quincy, the Upper Mississippi Valley, and the United States..." A tour of the museum exposes visitors to various materials used in construction throughout the years; diverse styles of buildings, such as the "cruciform cottages" and their cross-shaped floor plans; various periods of architecture; and photo exhibits depicting some of the period buildings once common in Quincy. The museum's second floor main gallery is called "Aspirations in Glass" and contains several stained glass windows salvaged from churches that were either demolished or were damaged beyond repair in one of Illinois' many storms.

Archaeological Wonder

The Dickson Mounds Museum in Lewistown is one of the country's most important on-site archaeological museums. The museum, which is founded atop a burial mound, was built around an excavation site first uncovered by Don Dickson in 1927. Although he unearthed the remains of these ancient residents, he did not remove the bones and surrounded the area with a tent. That first year alone garnered 40,000 visitors from around the world who were interested in this historic undertaking. The site was sold to the state after World War II, and aside from minimal interruption, it has operated as a museum since 1945.

Glitz and Glam

When it was built in 1927, at a price tag of $1.5 million, the Coronado Theatre in Rockford promised to be one of the most impressive movie palaces of its day. It didn't disappoint. Not only is the ambiance stunning, with chandeliers, artistic plaster work and magical ceilings, but since its first opening, the Coronado has hosted work from some of Hollywood's best. Among the big names are Bob Hope in "Roberta," the Marx Brothers, Rudy Vallee, Sammy Davis Jr., Liberace, Louis Armstrong, Phyllis Diller, Maurice Chevalier and Milton Berle.

In 1970, Willard N. Van Matre Jr. sold the Coronado Theatre to Kerasotes Theatres, and nine years later it was entered on the National Register of Historic Places. The theater is also listed on the State of Illinois Register of Historic Sites. Although it hasn't shown movies since 1984, the theater remained in the Kerasotes family until they donated it to Rockford on November 21, 1997. The Friends of the Coronado was eventually formed, $7 million was raised for renovations and another $7 million contributed by the city of Rockford. After 18 months of construction, the theater was reopened to the public in 2001.

TINY TREASURES

Just Super

The thriving metropolis of Metropolis, with a population of less than 7000 in 2002, is dubbed "Hometown of Superman"—and the city has a 15-foot bronze statue of the superhero to prove it. DC Comics officially handed the moniker to the community on January 21, 1972. In a whole-hearted effort to celebrate the honor, folks in Metropolis have lived the theme throughout the years. Their newspaper is named the *Metropolis Planet;* the city hosts a four-day-long Superman Festival every June; and the local chamber of commerce used to hand out packages of kryptonite.

Eight is Enough

Hamilton County is well known for a house that is no more. Sometime between 1850 and 1871, an eight-sided house was constructed, drawing interest and speculation from all who visited the area. It earned the name "The Old Octagonal House," though some sources suggest it should be dubbed the "Hexagon" or "Honeycomb" house because all the rooms were in the shape of hexagons. Sadly, the house was destroyed in a fire in 1973, but it continues to captivate imaginations to this day.

DID YOU KNOW?

The city of Salem, with its tree-lined streets, calls itself the "City of Trees."

Respect Your Elders

The oldest community in Illinois is Peoria. Settlers first came to the area in 1680 and built Fort Crevecoeur. A second fort, Fort Clark, was constructed in 1813 after the first burned, and in 1825, after Peoria County was organized, the fort was renamed Peoria.

Pumpkin Power
Dubbed the "Pumpkin Capital of the World," the community of Morton may be small, but when it comes to pumpkin pie, it's mighty. The Nestle/Libby's pumpkin-packing plant located in Morton produces an estimated 80 percent of the world's canned pumpkin. To celebrate the fact, an annual Pumpkin Festival is held every September, during pumpkin-picking season, of course!

TRUE ORIGINALS

One of a Kind

Rockford's Burpee Museum of Natural History is home to the most complete and well-preserved skeletons of a young *Tyrannosaurus rex* ever found. Affectionately known as "Jane," the T-rex was about 21 feet long and weighed 1500 pounds when she died at the estimated age of 11 years. She was discovered in 2001 in Montana.

Culinary First

Next time you whip up a potato salad with a slathering of creamy Miracle Whip, you can thank a Salem native for the recipe. According to local legend, the condiment had its beginnings at Max Crossett's Café and was known as "Max's X-tra Fine Salad Dressing." It was such a hit that Kraft bought the entrepreneur's recipe for $300 back in 1931, and it has been known as Kraft's Miracle Whip ever since.

Going Solo

It took two years of solitude, determination and steadfastness, but in 1992, William Pinkney made history. The retired marketing manager and public relations officer set out in 1990 on a solo trip, sailing around the world through some of the most treacherous seas. He was the first African American to complete this journey—one he shared with schoolchildren worldwide through the satellite-linked computer and shortwave radio he had on board. He was recognized for his efforts when he was awarded Chicago Yacht Club's Yachtsman of the Year in 1992, and in 1999, *Chicago* magazine heralded him as the Chicagoan of the Year.

Take Me Out to the Ball Game

"Get your hot dogs here!" The familiar cry immediately brings to mind the excitement of a good baseball game. And what better way to follow a great hot dog than with a box of Cracker Jack. The caramel-coated peanut and popcorn mixture started off with a molasses topping, was the brainchild of Chicagoan F.W. Rueckheim, and was first introduced in 1893 during Chicago's first World Fair. Rueckheim and his brother Louis worked on a formula for the topping that wouldn't be as sticky, and when they shared their concoction with a salesman in 1896, legend has it that he said, "That's crackerjack!" The snack became a quick favorite and was immortalized in 1908 when

Philly native Jack Norworth wrote "Buy me some peanuts and Cracker Jack" in the famous song "Take Me Out to the Ball Game."

One and Only

From the outside it looks like a quaint café with baskets over-flowing with flowers and welcoming signs offering cappuccino and espresso and, of course, ice-cold root beer. Located in Alto Pass, with a population of just a few hundred people, the Northwest Passage Root Beer Saloon boasts that it is the world's first, and likely only, root beer saloon. They offer "three micro-brewed draft root beers from St. Louis, Milwaukee and Chicago" on tap. Along with the root beer, you can indulge in any number of taste-tempting treats. And if you think you can get away with spiking your root beer, even just a little, think again. With more than 175 sets of antlers, mounted game fish and more than 150 ducks, geese and other birds on the walls, all eyes are on you!

Spicy Salutation
The state legislature made it official in 1993—Springfield is the "Chili Capital of the World."

Big Red Wagon
Radio Flyer Inc. of Chicago wanted to celebrate its 80th anniversary in 1997 in a big way, and what better way for the manufacturer of four-wheeled toys to do so than with a gigantic version of its famous creation. So Radio Flyer set out to build the world's largest wagon. Measuring 27 feet in length, 13 feet wide and weighing in at 15,000 pounds, the huge wagon can haul 75 energetic youngsters.

CELEBRATION SELECTION

Best Buddy

The name Johnny Gruelle might not be familiar to most, but his creation certainly is. Born in Arcola in 1880, Gruelle developed the original Raggedy Ann doll quite by accident when he added nothing more than a painted face to an old and dusty rag doll he gave his daughter. She loved her doll so much that she had it with her always. Wanting other girls to have such a positive experience, Gruelle created his own version and patented the Raggedy Ann doll on September 7, 1915. An artist and illustrator by profession, Gruelle then went on to create a series of books featuring what today has become a much-loved staple in every little girl's room. Since 1989, Arcola has hosted the Original Raggedy Ann and Andy Festival every June, drawing doll lovers and collectors alike from around the world. And while you're in town, check out the Raggedy Ann and Andy Museum where you'll discover more about the family behind the doll, get to see countless versions of the toy and learn about its development through the years.

Living Up to Its Name

In 1948, the Illinois legislature made it official—Kewanee was named "Hog Capital of the World." And if you have any doubt to the claim, just make your way to the town's downtown core. That's where you'll find Kewanee's mascot, the statue of a life-size pig peering through a brick structure, complete with a sign boasting its proud-as-a-pig status.

The town has worked hard to live up to its moniker. For a few years, folks in the area banded together for a daylong hog celebration in the summer or early fall. By 1955, the celebration had grown into an annual three-day festival called Kewanee Hog Days, and by 1959 it was decided to hold the event permanently every Labor Day. Today, along with a carnival and what folks down in Kewanee proudly call the "world's largest outdoor barbecue," those attending Hog Days can take in a Queen Pageant, the Hog Days Stampede, a Hoggatta Regatta featuring the best in radio-controlled model yachts and the muddiest volleyball game around.

Tissue Please!

If you're planning to take in this festival you might want to pack a tissue or two. Chances are at least once during your visit you'll find your eyes watering and nose running. As the self-proclaimed "Horseradish Capital of the World," Collinsville celebrates the spicy mustard-related root with its annual International Horseradish Festival in June. The event was first hosted in the 1980s in celebration of producing 60 percent of the world's horseradish. With no fat or cholesterol to worry about, horse-radish is the perfect condiment. And don't be surprised if locals ask whether you'd like horseradish with your burger. Just make sure you pick up a bottle of water or two as well.

Love Festival

Greenville is home to Greenville Christian College, so it's only natural the town hosts an annual Christian music festival. The Agape Music Festival is held each April at the Bond County Fairgrounds and boasts a long line-up of some of the best in Christian music talent. The event is sponsored by the college and has been running since 1977.

Sheer longevity is the reason the Old Settlers Days festival made it into this book. Nothing short of amazing community spirit could maintain this annual festival for well over 125 years, and that's exactly what Toulon has accomplished. Held each year since 1877, Old Settlers Days usually takes place the first weekend in August and features everything from tractor pulls and fish fries to kiddy parades, an ice cream social and music of all flavors.

Joining Forces

Toulon has its hand in another Stark County festival of note. The neighboring communities of Toulon, Bradford, Castleton, Lafayette, West Jersey and Wyoming, along with Indian Creek Vineyard, hold the area's annual Fall Festival on the third weekend of September. If you want to take in the craft tables, flea markets and entertainment, just mosey the roughly 70 miles from one community to the next and you won't miss a thing.

All That Glitters

Folks in Hardin County celebrate the success of a major industry in their area with the annual Hardin County Fluorspar Festival. The event has been held in Rosiclare the first weekend in October since 1965. Along with the usual food and craft vendors, the American Fluorite Museum uses the weekend to host an open house. Fluorite is often considered "the most colorful mineral in the world," widely coveted by jewelry makers and mineral collectors alike. It is also a component used to add flexibility to steel and is used in making pottery, plastics and glass.

DID YOU KNOW?

Over one million people in Illinois are of Polish descent, most of them dwelling in Chicago and the suburbs outside the city.

A Polish Presence

The annual Taste of Polonia festival—a celebration of Polish culture in Chicago—draws 30,000 celebrants each Labor Day weekend. Records indicate that the first Chicago Pole was a man by the name of Antoni Schermann, who came to the city in 1851. It is often said that Chicago is the second-largest Polish city in the world (with Warsaw, Poland's capital, being the only other city with more Polish people). Second City, indeed!

SPOOKY STUFF

You Better Not Go Alone

From a gangster hotspot to a ghostly relic, Vishnu has capti-vated ghost hunters and ghost town enthusiasts alike. The McDonough County ghost town was a holiday draw for Chicago gangsters in the early part of the 20th century. Legend has it that several untimely deaths as result of accidents and murders initiated hauntings in the area, which some believe continue to this day. The only problem is in getting to the spot. The remains of Vishnu are shrouded in woodland and fields, so if you want to see the three-story hotel, tombstones and other relics, you will need permission as they're now located on private property.

Wade in the Water

It looks much like any other stately mansion of the Old South, but John Hart Crenshaw didn't build the monstrosity on Hickory Hill for his family's or anyone else's enjoyment. Crenshaw House, or "The Old Slave House" as it came to be known, was built in 1842 to house black slaves who worked in the salt mines. It was work no one else wanted to do, and although it was against the law to own a slave in Illinois by that time, it wasn't against the law to borrow slaves from neighboring states. Crenshaw went one better; he actually abducted black slaves and forced them to work for him. At night the slaves were packed, sardine-style, in the attic of his stately looking house, and those less accommodating to his plans were said to be tortured there. The other freed slaves Crenshaw recaptured were resold to landowners in the southern states where slavery was still legal. Today, the entire house is believed haunted, but the area of the most supernatural activity is said to take place in the "attic of horrors."

Now You See It...

...and now you don't. To say the so-called ghost town of Coltonville is a mystery is an understatement. Not only is there next to no information on the community, which was thought to exist in DeKalb County in the late 19th century, it's hard to define exactly where it is. In fact, you'll have to wait for a heavy rain and then slush on through the fields to see the odd foundation or tombstone typically hidden by soil.

This and That

There's considerably more to see in Orchard Place in Cook County as far as ghost towns are concerned. Folks primarily of German persuasion settled the railway town and farming community in 1833. It must have been a fairly solid community because, as recently as 1948, a new school was built. But today, aside from the vacant school, the only other things to survive are an assortment of old farmhouses, barns and two cemeteries.

LARGER THAN LIFE

Holy Hot Dogs!

Follow Route 66 into downtown Atlanta and sooner or later you'll come across a 19-foot tall Paul Bunyan statue holding a mammoth hot dog, mustard and all.

Gemini Giant

Paul Bunyan takes on a space-aged feel as the Gemini Giant, mascot to the Launching Pad Drive-In Restaurant since 1965. Located on Route 66 in Wilmington, the 28-foot tall, helmet-wearing, spaceship-wielding wonder rises above most of the surrounding buildings.

The Tire Guy

Route 66 boasts yet another giant mascot in the form of the Lauterbach Tire Man. This towering giant is located on Springfield's Wabash Avenue and welcomes patrons to the Lauterbach Tire and Auto Service.

Billboard Art

There's real skill involved in painting billboard signs, and a group known as the Letterheads dedicates its spare time to reviving and preserving these outdoor works of art, many of which have considerable historic value. Downtown Atlanta prides itself in six such restored murals easily spotted along Route 66:

☞ Atlanta celebrates its central location on the famed highway, which is the midway point between St. Louis and Chicago, with a 20-x-6-foot mural entitled "Atlanta—Midway on Illinois' Mother Road." The mural was designed by Bill Diaz of Pontiac and completed in June 2003.

☛ Bill Diaz also recreated the J.M. Judy and Sons mural. As with the original painted in 1890, the current 70-x-15-foot mural advertises the grocery, along with "Queensware (china), notions and musical merchandise."

☛ The Palms Grill Café mural recaptures a time when a steady stream of hungry customers passed through the doors of the Palms Grill Café between 1934 and the late 1960s. The café also doubled as a Greyhound bus stop, and if you were looking to hop on board, you just had to make sure the light above the café door was on.

☛ For only 50 cents, the Wisteria Café and Confectionery served up homemade chicken dinners from "noon to night during fair week." The special suppers were just one of many draws to this hotspot in the 1920s. Nancy Bennett, using some of the company's original ad copy, designed a mural commemorating the Wisteria.

☛ Atlanta's volunteer firefighters are saluted in the Firehouse Tribute mural created by Stephan "Conman" Connor.

☛ If you didn't know it before, Dave "Herbie" Estes' re-creation of the original Reisch Beer mural makes the claim loud and clear—"Reisch Beer Will Give You Health and Strength!" The original mural, though seriously faded since it was painted in 1894, is still faintly visible on the building that once sold the product.

HISTORICAL HAPPENINGS

Way Back When

Native Americans have inhabited Illinois since 8000 BC, and the largest settlement before Europeans came into the picture was in present-day Collinsville, where the Mississippian culture thrived in Cahokia from 1300 to about 1400 AD. At its peak, Cahokia was the largest urban area north of Mexico, with some archaeologists estimating that it had as many as 40,000 people. If the estimate is accurate, that would make Cahokia bigger than any U.S. city until 1800, when Philadelphia surpassed 40,000. One more thing, Cahokia is home to the largest human-made mound in North America, Monk's Mound. It got its name years after the Native Americans constructed it, when Irish Christian monks came to reside nearby and garden in the area.

Jolliet and Marquette

In 1673, French explorers Louis Jolliet and Jacques Marquette became the first known Europeans to enter and map the Mississippi River. They made it to Arkansas and returned back up the river, where Native Americans showed them the way to Lake Michigan through the Illinois River. This event was the beginning of the modern history of Illinois. Jolliet and Marquette are also known as the first Europeans to spend time in the area that is now Chicago.

Changing Hands

Illinois' journey to statehood was a rather complicated one, so buckle your seatbelts before reading on. Following Jolliet and Marquette's discovery, the Illinois area would become a part of the French empire until 1763, when, as a result of the French and Indian War, France ceded all lands east of the Mississippi to Britain. It was then known as Illinois Country. During the Revolutionary War, the American troops captured Kaskaskia, which was the seat of Britain's Illinois territory, and Illinois briefly became a county of Virginia. In 1787, the area became part of the Northwest Territory, and in 1800 it became a part of the Indiana Territory. Finally, in 1809, Congress established Illinois Territory, which originally contained parts of present-day Wisconsin, Minnesota and Michigan. But it was not until 1818 that Illinois officially entered the union as the 21st state, with Kaskaskia as its capital. Phew!

Chicago almost ended up in Wisconsin—it's true! While working as a territorial delegate for the U.S. Congress, Nathaniel Pope had the presence of mind to lobby for the adjustment of Illinois' northern border. Originally, Illinois' slice of land was only 10 miles north of the southern tip of Lake Michigan, but Pope realized the importance of a large body of water for food and transportation purposes. He convinced the government to expand Illinois 41 miles farther north by arguing that it was necessary in order to connect Illinois with the eastern states of the union. Pope County, in the northeastern corner of the state that was saved by Pope, is aptly named after him.

The First Guv'nor

Shadrach Bond (1773–1832) was elected governor of Illinois in 1818, making him the first in the history of the state. He served until 1822. Bond County, in the southwestern part of the state near St. Louis, and Governor Bond Lake, near Greenville, are both named after him.

Martyr of the Press

Elijah Parish Lovejoy (1802–37) was a journalist and minister who had some unfortunate luck. Originally from Maine, Lovejoy moved to St. Louis in 1834 and became the pastor of a Presbyterian church. He also started a newspaper called the

St. Louis Observer, which advocated the abolition of slavery. After his printing press was destroyed by a mob angry over his coverage of a lynching, Lovejoy crossed the river to Alton, where he continued to advocate the end of slavery with the *Alton Observer*. His press was seized three different times and thrown into the Mississippi River, but he refused to be intimidated. Finally, on November 7, 1837, after the publisher received another printing press from the Ohio Anti-Slavery Society, a local mob of slave-owners attacked Lovejoy and shot him dead. He's remembered as a martyr to the freedom of speech and press and a pioneer of the abolitionist movement.

The Black Hawk War

The Sauk and Fox were Native American tribes who lived in northern Illinois and southern Wisconsin. As American pioneers headed west during the early 1800s, the land of these tribes became threatened. In 1830, a U.S. treaty was imposed, forcing the tribes to leave and relocate to Iowa. After a difficult winter and many problems producing crops, the tribes returned to their original area in northern Illinois in 1832, led by Chief Black Hawk. The tribes hoped to forge an alliance with the settlers who had taken their land. Instead, the settlers organized a militia. Black Hawk surrendered, waving a peace flag, but his gestures were misinterpreted by the wild militia, who attacked the Natives. Thus began the Black Hawk War of 1832, which lasted almost four months.

In all, 70 American settlers died, as well as 1000 of Black Hawk's people. Eventually Black Hawk surrendered and was imprisoned. After meeting with President Andrew Jackson, he was sent to live in Iowa with his surviving relatives. He maintained dignity and humility in defeat, saying to those who came to settle his former land, "The Rock River country was a beautiful country. I loved my towns and my cornfields, for they were home to my people. I fought for it. It is now yours. Keep it as we did."

Future presidents Abraham Lincoln and Zachary Taylor, as well as Jefferson Davis (who would later become the president of the Confederacy during the Civil War), all played various roles during the Black Hawk War. Lincoln served in the militia, although he never engaged in any combat. Taylor led troops under Henry Atkinson, who was the overall commander of the war. Davis escorted the captured Black Hawk and other leaders of the Sauk and Fox tribes to Jefferson Barracks (a military post near St. Louis) after they surrendered.

Before It Had Such Broad Shoulders

Chicago hasn't always been the powerhouse city it is today, of course. It was incorporated as a town (population 350) on August 12, 1833. On March 4, 1837, the city charter was enacted into law. The city had grown to 4170 people in the space of four years, and William Butler Ogden was chosen the first mayor of Chicago. Here are some notable dates from the early years of this fine American city:

- 1837: C.D. Peacock Jewelers is founded, the oldest Chicago business still operating today.

- 1847: The first issue of the *Chicago Tribune* is printed.

- 1848: The Illinois and Michigan Canal is completed, helping establish Chicago as a major U.S. transportation hub.

- 1848: Telegraph lines reach Chicago.

- 1848: The Chicago Board of Trade is established, allowing grains and livestock to be bought and sold on paper.

- 1851: Northwestern University, the city's first university of higher education, is founded.

- 1855: Newly elected mayor Levi D. Boone organizes the city's first police department.

- 1860: Chicago hosts its first political convention; the Republicans nominate Abraham Lincoln for the presidency.

- 1863: The first hospital in Illinois, Mercy Hospital, opens in Chicago.

- 1867: Construction on the Chicago Water Tower begins.

- 1871: The Great Chicago Fire.

- 1885: The Home Insurance Building—the world's first sky-scraper—is erected on LaSalle Street in downtown Chicago.

DID YOU  KNOW?

Peoria is widely considered the oldest city in Illinois, dating back to French exploration in the late 1600s.

Union Dues
During the American Civil War (1861–65), Illinois fought for the northern states of the Union (against the Confederate South), contributing somewhere around 250,000 troops. No battles were fought in the state, though the towns of Cairo and Mound City in the southern part of Illinois were important supply bases for the Union troops. Camp Butler, near Springfield, and Camp Douglas, near Chicago, both served as training camps for the troops as well as POW camps for captured Confederates.

The Great Chicago Fire

On October 8, 1871, a fire started in downtown Chicago. It didn't stop for two days, and when all was said and done, 90,000 Chicago residents were homeless and 18,000 buildings had been destroyed in the space of about four square miles. Estimates range between 200 and 300 fire-related deaths. Mrs. O'Leary's cow kicking over a lantern in a barn did not start the

fire, as legend has it. In 1893, Michael Ahern, the journalist responsible for the cow story, admitted that he had made it up because it made for colorful copy.

Only a handful of buildings in the fire's path survived, including Water Tower Place, which still sits in the middle of downtown Chicago amidst modern skyscrapers and is the only surviving structure still standing.

DID YOU KNOW?

On October 8, the same day the Great Chicago Fire started, Peshtigo, Wisconsin (400 miles north of Chicago) suffered a prairie fire that destroyed 1.5 million acres of land and killed between 1200 and 2500 people, making it the deadliest fire in American history. This coincidence prompted some physicists and engineers to suggest that the fires were the result of a meteor shower.

Haymarket Riot

During the late 19th century, Chicago was a hotbed of labor unrest and anarchism, and all of it came to a head in 1886. On May 1, a labor strike was held in the city as part of a movement for an eight-hour workweek; 90,000 Chicagoans participated. Two days later, as the strike continued on, a fight broke out outside the McCormick Harvesting Machine Company plant when replacement workers attempted to cross the picket line. The police intervened, killing one of the strikers and wounding many others, which caused widespread outrage among the city's united workers.

The following day, May 4, a protest meeting was called at Haymarket Square, on the corner of Randolph and Des Plaines streets. Anarchists had distributed fliers claiming that the police had intentionally attacked the strikers over business interests. Toward the end of the rally, as police attempted to disperse the crowd, a bomb exploded, causing mass hysteria. In the end, seven police officers and at least four workers were killed. Sixty officers were wounded. Eight radicals and anarchists were rounded up over the next few days and eventually brought to trial and convicted, though the bomb thrower was never identified. International Workers' Day (sometimes referred to as May Day) is observed every year on May 1 in honor of the Haymarket Riot.

A large bronze statue was erected in Haymarket Square in 1889 in commemoration of the event. On the 41st anniversary of the riot, a streetcar jumped off its tracks and crashed into the statue. In 1969, the monument was blown up; the city repaired the damages, but it was blown up again the following year, reportedly by radical left-wing group the Weather Underground. In 1972, the statue was moved again to a safer spot: the Chicago Police Academy.

Mother Jones

Mary Harris Jones (1837–1930) was a tiny woman (barely five feet tall) who was born in Ireland and became one of the fiercest labor activists in America. She spent most of her professional years in Chicago, but was raised in Toronto, where she learned dressmaking and teaching skills. "Mother Jones," as she was called, overcame tremendous tragedies to become the great leader she was: in 1867, while working in Tennessee, her husband and all four of her children died during a yellow fever epidemic, and in 1871, she lost all her possessions in the Great Chicago Fire. Nevertheless, she forged on, taking an interest in organizing labor unions, especially those of coal miners. She spent the rest of her life traveling the country and participating in strikes, correcting what she considered wrongs against the poor and downtrodden workers of the U.S. She once said of herself, "I'm not a humanitarian, I'm a hell-raiser."

Hull House

Jane Addams (1860–1932) was born in Cedarville, but Chicago is where she opened Hull House, a settlement house that became the most famous and respected of its kind in the U.S. Hull House provided a place where immigrants in the city could go to better themselves through night school (a concept that Addams pioneered and is a common practice today for workers seeking an education) and various social activities. Hull House also played a significant political role in the city, advocating for immigration and child labor reform and workers' rights. For her efforts, Addams was awarded the Nobel Peace Prize in 1931.

The River That Flows Backward

The Chicago River was not the most popular body of water in Illinois in the late 1880s. For one, it had failed to stop the spread of the Great Chicago Fire in 1871, much to the chagrin of residents of the city's north side. And large amounts of human waste regularly flowed into the river, which in turn flowed into Lake Michigan, the source of Chicago's drinking water. To fix this, civil engineers reversed the flow of the water by building a 28-mile canal in 1900. The river now flows from the lake into the Mississippi River basin. The project was considered one of the great feats of modern engineering and the largest municipal earth-moving project ever completed.

DID YOU KNOW?

Every St. Patrick's Day, the Chicago River is dyed green. A Chicago plumber came up with the idea in 1962. Interestingly, the dye looks orange when it's first applied to the river, but then transforms to a brilliant, emerald shade of green when mixed with the water. The first year the river was dyed, 100 pounds of dye were used, and the river remained green for a week. The next year, they used 50 pounds, and it stayed green for three days. Finally, it was determined that 25 pounds was all that was needed to keep the water green for one day.

OFF THE WALL AND ON THE MAP

Alton

The city was named after the son of Rufus Easton, a founding father of the town. Easton operated a passenger ferry line on the Mississippi River and was also the first postmaster of St. Louis.

Aurora

This city bills itself as the "City of Lights" because it was one of the first cities in the United States to install electric street lights, all the way back in 1881. It's said that the name Aurora was chosen because the Northern Lights (*aurora borealis*) appeared in the night sky on the eve of the most popular festival in the area. Aurora's official colors are blue and green, a tribute to the colors that flash in the night sky during this phenomenon. Also of note regarding this Chicago suburb is that "Wayne's World," about two 20-something men (Mike Myers and Dana Carvey) who broadcast a cable-access show from their basement, is based in Aurora. The hugely popular *Saturday Night Live* sketch was later made into two major motion pictures.

Bartlett

Founded by Luther Bartlett, a Massachusetts native, and incorporated in 1891, the village of Bartlett actually lies in three different counties: Cook, Kane and DuPage. In 2004, the largest traditional Hindu Mandir in the United States opened its doors in Bartlett—the BAPS Shri Swaminarayan Mandir, which covers 22,400 square feet. Many of its marble and limestone carvings were shipped in from India, and there are 16 domes, 151 pillars and 75 ceilings with 39 different designs in the Mandir. Quite an impressive architectural feat.

Belleville

Although "Belleville" is French for "beautiful city," a large majority of the townsfolk—some figures put it as high as 90 percent—are of German ancestry. This southern Illinois city (former home of the Stag Beer Brewery) also claims to be home to the longest Main Street in America, at nine miles.

Carlinville

This town is named after former Illinois governor Thomas Carlin (1838–42).

Colchester

During the 1850s, coal was discovered in the area now known as Colchester. However, the "Col" in "Colchester" is not simply an ethnic variation of the word "coal." That was just a happy coincidence of homophones. The town was actually named after Colchester, England, a town that claims to be the oldest in Britain.

Decatur

The city is named after Stephen Decatur Jr., a military hero from the War of 1812. At age 25, Decatur was the youngest officer ever to reach the rank of captain in the history of the United States Navy.

Effingham

Named after Edward Effingham, a general in the British army who refused to fight against the American colonies during the Revolutionary War.

Elgin

James and Hezekiah Gifford named the town after a Scottish hymn, "The Song of Elgin." Elgin is heralded as having fine architecture, and at one time had the largest concentration of cobblestone houses outside of Rochester, New York. Today, Elgin is one of the fastest growing cities in Illinois. In 2005, Mayor Ed Schock was quoted as saying that in 40 years, Elgin would be the second-largest city in the state—a pretty lofty goal but not altogether crazy in light of the praise Elgin has received. Consider this: in 2002, the National Civic League awarded their prestigious All-America City Award to Elgin. The award is given annually to 10 U.S. cities whose citizens "work together to identify and tackle community-wide challenges and achieve uncommon results." Also, a 1997 issue of *Money Magazine* hailed the city as a microcosm of the United States.

Galena

The mineral galena was mined and used by Native Americans for the purposes of body painting. The land the city was built on had a rich supply of this resource, thus the name. Galena is still home to Vinegar Hill Lead Mine, which is the only lead mine in the state open for tours.

DID YOU  KNOW?

Eight-five percent of Galena's buildings are in a National Register Historical District. Also, the 18th president of the United States, Ulysses S. Grant, lived in Galena. He worked as an assistant in a leather shop owned by his father before going off to become a general in the Civil War. Grant waited for the 1868 presidential election results while staying at a friend's home in Galena.

Galesburg

Named after George Washington Gale, a Presbyterian minister from New York who had aspirations of opening a manual labor college. The institution is now known as Knox College, and it is still in Galesburg.

Golconda

Originally called Sarahsville, the name was changed to Golconda (after the ancient city of Golkonda in India) in 1817. Some 13,000 Cherokee Natives passed through the town during the infamous Trail of Tears of the late 1830s.

Gurnee

Although he never lived in the actual town (and quite possibly never even stepped foot in the area), the town is named after former Chicago mayor Walter S. Gurnee, who served from 1851 to 1853. Gurnee has historically been known as a stopover between the cities of Chicago and Milwaukee.

Hoffman Estates, a suburb of Chicago, is home to *Den Danske Pioneer*, the nation's oldest Danish American newspaper dating back to 1872.

Jacksonville

The origin of the name is disputed. Town officials believe it was named after Andrew Jackson, the seventh president of the United States and, at the time of the city's founding, a recent hero of the Battle of New Orleans in the War of 1812. However, an urban legend exists wherein a young slave boy got lost in the area and came upon a group of men driving stakes into the ground. He asked for directions and told the men that his name was A.W. Jackson. The men told the boy that they were laying out a town and that they would name it after him because he was the first of his race in the area. It's likely that they only told the boy this because the town was already to be named Jacksonville. In any case, A.W. Jackson—who later in life confirmed the story—lived to be the first pastor of Mount Emory Baptist Church as well as Jacksonville's first African American alderman.

Joliet

Originally called Juliet (some say after one of the town's settler's daughters; some say after the heroine of Shakespeare's famous play *Romeo and Juliet*—Romeoville is the name of a town in the same county), the name was later changed to Joliet, in honor of the French Canadian explorer Louis Jolliet, who visited the town in 1673.

Kaskaskia

Oh, how the mighty have fallen. Now an island with only nine inhabitants (as of the 2000 census), Kaskaskia used to be the capital of Illinois in 1818. (That honor was given to Vandalia in 1820, and later to Springfield in 1837.) In 1881, a flood divided Kaskaskia, creating Kaskaskia Island, which is one of the only Illinois communities that is actually located west of the Mississippi River.

Moline

French for "City of Mills," the city was so named because, well, there were a lot of mills in the area when Moline was founded in 1848.

Monmouth

A draw from a hat is responsible for this town's moniker. Three possible names were submitted: Kosciusko, Isabella and Monmouth. "Kosciusko" was drawn, but it was deemed too difficult to spell and pronounce, and so "Monmouth," the next name drawn, was the winner. The town is the birthplace of one of the most famous gunslingers of the Old West, Wyatt Earp, who was born at 406 S. 3rd Street in 1848.

Nauvoo

In 1838, the religious group now known as the Latter-Day Saints (or Mormons) was forced out of Missouri and ended up in Illinois. It's there that they founded Nauvoo (which was believed to be Hebrew for "to be beautiful"), a town located in a swampy area on the Mississippi River, just north of the Missouri border. Mormons and new converts to the religion flooded into the area, which was proclaimed the new home of the faith. They quickly became a powerful force to be reckoned with in Illinois. Joseph Smith, founder and president of the church, was not only the city's mayor but the general of its militia and the head of the municipal court. In many ways, the growing town of Nauvoo increasingly started to resemble a theocracy, much to the distaste of neighboring cities.

In 1844, some disgruntled former members of the church published a newspaper criticizing Smith and his practices; Smith responded by ordering the paper and the press destroyed. Once news of this got out, Illinois governor Thomas Ford stepped in and proposed a trial (by a non-Mormon jury) for Smith in nearby Carthage. Smith—who by this time was a very unpopular figure outside of his faith—agreed to be taken into custody during the trial and was guaranteed complete safety by Ford. That didn't happen: an angry mob rushed the jailhouse on June 27, 1844, and he was shot as he attempted to leap out a window, falling to his death. It is widely believed that Governor Ford was aware of the impending attack and approved of it, as the Mormons had posed a number of problems for him over the years.

In December 1844, the Mormon charter of Nauvoo was repealed by the Illinois legislature, and in 1846 the Mormons began their exodus to Salt Lake City, where their headquarters remain today.

Olney

Olney was founded in 1841, is the county seat of Richland County and is known for its large population of white squirrels. These odd little creatures have been granted the right-of-way in all Olney streets, and if you're ever driving around the town, keep an eye out for them: it'll cost you $200 if you accidentally (or purposely) run one of them over. By the way, if you are

looking to squirrel watch, the best time is early in the morning. It's estimated that approximately 200 white squirrels wander around the town, down from nearly 1000 in the 1940s.

Palestine

French explorer Jean LaMotte reportedly named this town in 1678 after declaring that it resembled "the land of milk and honey." It was given a charter in 1811, making it one of the oldest towns in Illinois. Palestine was home to two history-making women: Mary Ann "Auntie" Gogin, whom town residents claim was the first woman in Illinois to run and manage her own business, and Elizabeth "Betsey" Reed, the only woman in the state's history to be executed by hanging (she poisoned her husband by putting arsenic in his tea in 1844). Reed also attempted to burn the jailhouse she was kept in to the ground and almost succeeded. In July 2007, Palestine debuted the first annual Betsey Reed Festival, a weekend with events such as coffin races and a dramatic retelling of the woman's story at the local opera house. The slogan of the weekend? "Come Hang Around Palestine with Betsey." Maybe a little insensitive…but we kinda like it.

Pekin

In 1829, an auction was held for the area of land that is now known as Pekin, and it was awarded to four men. One of the men was named Nathan Cromwell, and it was his wife who named the town, after Peking (now Beijing), the capital city of China, which at the time was sometimes referred to as "Pekin." Today, the city is home to the Mechanical Baking Company, which produces and sells an authentic hardtack biscuit, similar to the kind that soldiers ate during the Civil War. (They're popular among Civil War re-enactors.) The biscuits are so hard that you need a hard rock (or perhaps the butt of a re-enactor's rifle) to break them up. Mmm…

Peoria

Named after a Native American Illiniwek tribe common to the area. In the tribe's language, *peoria* means "comes carrying a pack on his back."

The common question, "Will it play in Peoria?" originated during the vaudeville era of the 1920s, when new stage shows were booked in Peoria to judge audience reaction. Peoria was considered an effective litmus test for all heart-of-America towns.

Princeton

According to local legend, Princeton was christened by drawing names from a hat. The three founders of the town couldn't agree on a name, and so each wrote their preferred name on a slip of paper, dropped it in a hat and had a blindfolded stranger reach in and pick one out. The winner, John Musgrove (originally from New Jersey), chose the name Princeton as a tribute to the city in the Garden State that he loved most. Princeton was later a stop on the Underground Railroad during the 19th century.

DID YOU KNOW?

Princeton was known as the City of Elms because of the large number of elm trees in the region. However, Dutch elm disease wiped out nearly every elm tree in the city in the 1950s. The city's new slogan is "Where Tradition Meets Progress," but some still call it by its original nickname.

Quincy

Also known as the "Gem City," Quincy was named after John Quincy Adams, the sixth president of the United States. Quincy is also the county seat of Adams County, similarly named after the president.

Shelbyville

Founded in 1829, Shelbyville was named after Isaac Shelby, a hero of the Revolutionary War. This charming little town is also where Josephine Garis Cochrane invented the dishwasher in 1886.

Springfield

What is now the capital of Illinois was originally known as Calhoun, named after John C. Calhoun, a senator from South Carolina. But Calhoun (the man) wasn't popular enough for long enough, and the town was renamed "Springfield" in 1832. Natives of the city allege that their own Cozy Dog Drive-In is the birthplace of what is now known as the corn dog.

Wheaton

Founded by Warren and Jesse Wheaton, the town is said to have more churches per capita than any other town in America. In 1873, a man by the name of Charles Barnes opened a book business from his home in the town. Years later, his son took over the business and, along with G. Clifford Noble, established Barnes & Noble books in New York City. Today, it's a $5 billion company with 55,000 employees. And there's an outlet in Wheaton.

KEEPIN' IT REAL

Chicago vs. the Rest of the State

In much the same way New Yorkers have a tendency to forget about life outside of their city limits, Chicagoans are often guilty of thinking of Illinois as having two parts: the part that's in Chicago, and "downstate," which usually means any place in the state that is not in Chicago. Nearly half of Illinois' population resides in Cook County (the Chicago metropolitan area, and the second-largest county by population in the U.S., behind Los Angeles County, in California). In light of this, it can be difficult to pin down what passes for an average Illinois lifestyle when the state contains the extreme poles of big-city cosmopolitanism and some of the most salt-of-the-earth rural regions you're likely to find in America.

Chicago: Vice City

The Windy City, like all large urban hubs across the world, is the kind of place that can indulge nearly every bad habit imaginable. Drinks, sex, drugs: you name it, you can find it somewhere in this vast lakeside metropolis.

Drink Up

Drinking is a part of the Chicago lifestyle, and the city has more bars per capita than both New York and Los Angeles. It's nearly impossible to walk down a city street without being beckoned by a vintage Old Style sign or a sidewalk chalkboard advertising cheap drink specials. And according to a study from the Substance Abuse and Mental Health Services Administration, Chicago has the highest binge-drinking rate in the country, at 25.7 percent.

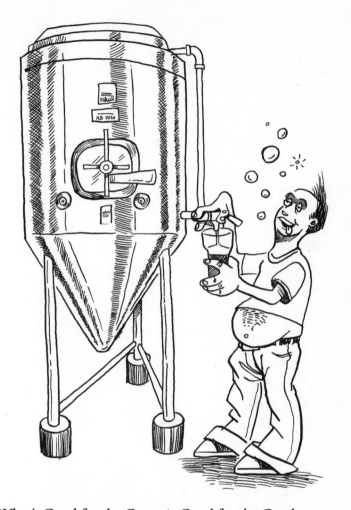

What's Good for the Goose is Good for the Gander
Mega-popular (in Illinois at least), Goose Island Brewery calls
Chicago home. Started in 1988 by founder John Hall, the brew-
ery distributes over 50 finely crafted beers to 15 states in the
U.S. The beers have names such as Honkers Ale, Demolition,
and 312 Urban Wheat—which is named after an area code in
Chicago. There's also two Goose Island bars in Chicago, one of
which is just a stone's throw from Wrigley Field.

Wine Country?

Illinois isn't necessarily the first place that comes to mind when the subject of wine comes up, but the state has got its own thing goin' on. Some wine factoids:

☛ There are around 70 wineries across the state of Illinois.

☛ The Illinois wine industry produces 500,000 gallons of wine per year.

☛ More than 300 vineyards across the state span over 1000 acres that produce grapes for the state's wineries.

☛ Somewhat ironically, Nauvoo—once home to the famously strict non-drinkers, the Latter-Day Saints—is known throughout the state for its fine wines.

☛ In 2005, Governor Blagojevich declared September "Illinois Wine Month," as a way of recognizing the growing wine industry in the state—it now brings in around $250 million annually for Illinois.

PIED NOIR

Put That Out!

Smokers in Illinois are having a rough time these days. In 2006, the Cook County tax on cigarettes nearly doubled, to $2 a pack, making Chicago the city with the highest tobacco tax in the United States. If you include county, city, state and federal taxes, it adds up to over $4 worth of taxes per pack—meaning that a pack usually costs somewhere between $7 and $8!

And as of January 1, 2008, Illinois smokers will have to take it outside. On July 23, 2007, Governor Rod Blagojevich signed into law a smoking ban preventing public smoking throughout the entire state, making it the 19th state in the union to pass such legislation. Every restaurant, bar and bingo hall in the Land of Lincoln will be smoke-free.

Holy Meth!

The methamphetamine epidemic has hit the Midwestern U.S. hard in the past decade, and Illinois is far from immune to its destructive effects. Some rather depressing facts about the use of this dirty drug:

☞ As is the case elsewhere, meth use is especially prevalent in rural areas of the state, with studies indicating that over 80 percent is found outside of large cities.

☞ One reason why meth use is common in rural areas is because of the abundance of anhydrous ammonia on farms. The agricultural community embraces its use because it is an effective, low-cost nitrogen fertilizer; however, it is also a key ingredient in the production of meth.

☞ Between 2000 and 2005, authorities seized 4509 meth labs.

☞ A law went into effect in January 2006 that imposed stricter standards for customers purchasing cold and sinus products containing pseudoephedrine, or PSE (a key ingredient in manufacturing meth). All such products are now

kept behind the counter, and consumers must show identi-
fication and sign a confidential log when purchasing these
items. Also, there is a two-package limit for all transactions.

Sexually Speaking

Some perhaps not-so-appealing facts about the sex lives of
Illinois residents (as of 2004):

☞ The teen birthrate per 1000 people was 40.2.

☞ The rate of chlamydia per 100,000 people was 397.7,
seventh highest in the nation.

☞ The gonorrhea rate per 100,000 people was 157.5, 11th
highest in the nation.

☞ The syphilis rate was 12.6 per 100,000 people, 13th highest in the country.

☞ The HIV testing rate was 46.1 percent, just above the
national average.

DID YOU KNOW?

In 2004, Illinois had a divorce rate of 2.6 per 1000 people,
which puts them in the top five in the nation (that's a good
thing—less divorce than the other states, not more).

The Gay-Friendly City

Chicago has a thriving gay community, much of which is centered around the Boystown neighborhood north of downtown.
In fact, Boystown was the first officially recognized gay village
in the United States. Long-time mayor Richard M. Daley has
been vocal about supporting gay marriage, and it is estimated
that the Chicagoland area is home to a population of some
300,000 lesbian/gay/bisexual/transgender (LGBT) residents.

In addition to hosting the 2006 Gay Games, Chicago is also home to the Gay and Lesbian Hall of Fame, and the *Windy City Times*, one of the nation's top LGBT newspapers.

God's People

When it comes to a popularity contest between religions, Protestants take home the trophy for the largest religious group, at 49 percent. But Roman Catholics, who comprise a solid 30 percent of the population, are giving them a run for their money. A full 80 percent of Illinois residents consider themselves Christians, while 16 percent say they're not religious, and four percent fall in the category of "Other" (Jewish, Muslim, Hindu).

TASTY TREATS

Deep Dish Pizza

Just exactly who was responsible for the creation of the first deep dish pizza is the subject of much debate, but one thing is widely agreed upon: it was created at Pizzeria Uno in Chicago sometime in the early 1940s. Among those who claim inventor status are Ike Sewell, owner of Pizzeria Uno; Rudy Malnati, a lowly chef at the restaurant; and Ric Riccardo, a partner of Sewell who later opened Riccardo's restaurant.

Real Chicago-style pizza generally is made using a rich, buttery crust formed by a deep-dish pan. The crust is then filled with cheese—always gooey—and whatever toppings are desired (Italian sausage, peppers, mushrooms, onions and pepperoni are recommended), and lastly, chunky tomato sauce is spread across the top. Bold souls might try eating it with their hands, but good luck—a knife and fork will make things a lot easier.

Some famous Chicago-style pizza peddlers:

☛ Chicago's

☛ Connie's

☛ Edwardo's

☛ Gino's

☛ Lou Malnati's (opened by one of Rudy's sons, and now an Illinois chain with over 25 locations)

☛ Giordano's

☛ Pizano's (owned by Rudy Malnati's son, Rudy Jr.)

☛ Pizzeria Uno (now an international chain with 216 restaurants in 32 states)

The Hot Dog Capital of the Universe

Chicagoans take their hot dogs seriously, and they have their own special take on how to make 'em. First of all, you've got to have Vienna beef and a steamed poppy seed bun. Then, in the following order, add:

☛ Yellow mustard

☛ Bright green relish

☛ Chopped onions

☛ Two tomato wedges

☛ Pickle spear

☛ Two sport peppers

☛ A dash of celery salt

And don't forget: when you're making the dog, dress the meat itself, not the bun. Oh yeah, and one more thing: NO KETCHUP! Chicago hot dog connoisseurs frown upon ketchup as a condiment for their dogs, insisting that the flavor overpowers the taste—and therefore the purity—of the dog. In fact, the National Hot Dog & Sausage Council (yes, such a group exists) explicitly states that those over the age of 18 are not to participate in the use of this red menace.

If you follow the above instructions, you'll have a real Chicago dog "with the works." The dog is also referred to as "dragged through the garden," because of the presence of so many vegetables.

DID YOU KNOW?

☛ There are more hot dog joints in Chicago than there are McDonald's, Burger Kings, and Wendy's combined.

☛ Over 80 percent of the 1800 hot dog vendors in Chicago serve Vienna beef.

☛ O'Hare International Airport in Chicago is the world's largest retailer of hot dogs, with travelers purchasing two million dogs per year.

☛ The average hot dog is consumed in 6.1 bites.

Here's a handful of world-class hot dog joints in the Prairie State:

   ☛ Gold Coast Dogs (Chicago)

☛ Michael's Chicago Style Red Hots (Highland Park)

☛ Mustard's Last Stand (Evanston)

☛ Poochie's (Skokie)

☞ Portillo's (Chicago)

☞ Superdawg (Chicago)

☞ The Wiener's Circle (Chicago)

Billions and Billions Served

Arguably the most recognized symbol in the entire world, the Golden Arches of McDonald's have quite a history with the great state of Illinois. The first McDonald's was actually opened in San Bernardino, California, by Dick and Mac McDonald in 1948. In 1954, a milkshake machine salesman from Oak Brook, Illinois, named Ray Kroc visited San Bernardino and was inspired by the brothers' assembly line system for making hamburgers. Kroc soon partnered with the two and started his own McDonald's franchise in Des Plaines, Illinois, on April 15, 1955, which the McDonald's Corporation now considers to be the "first" McDonald's (in fact it was the ninth location and opened for business 15 years after the first McDonald's opened for business). In 1961, Kroc bought out Dick and Mac's share of the company for $2.7 million, and the rest, as they say, is history.

What's that? You want some delicious facts about Mickey D's? Well, it just so happens that we've got a bunch of 'em:

☞ McDonald's is headquartered in Oak Brook, Illinois.

☞ McDonald's serves approximately 54 million people worldwide per day.

☞ Nearly one in eight workers in the U.S. has at one point been employed by McDonald's.

☞ Kroc is credited with one of the most annoying sayings in the history of the English language: "If you've got time to lean, you've got time to clean."

☞ Until 2006, McDonald's owned a majority stake in Chipotle, the popular Mexican restaurant.

☛ In Salen, Sweden, there is a McDonald's with a ski-through window.

☛ Not exactly shocking: McDonald's is the world's largest purchaser of beef.

☛ According to the 2001 book *Fast Food Nation*, 96 percent of U.S. schoolchildren can successfully identify Ronald McDonald.

☛ Ronald McDonald is formally recognized by the company as "Chief Happiness Officer."

Hot Eats and Cool Treats

What is now Dairy Queen began in Kankakee in 1938, when Sherwood Noble gave a test-run to a new "soft-serve" dairy product that his friend J.F. McCullough, and his son, had come up with. The product was sold as an "all-you-can-eat for 10 cents," and in two hours, Noble's ice cream store sold 1600 servings. Obviously they hit on something. The first "DQ," as it came to be called, opened in Joliet in 1940, and today it's one of the largest franchises in the entire world, selling not only ice cream treats but also hamburgers, hot dogs and other classic American items.

INDUSTRIES OF ILLINOIS

Money Talks

In many ways, Illinois is thriving, fiscally speaking. Much of the state's wealth is obviously centered in and around Chicago, but the downstate folks bring home the bacon as well. Here is an assortment of info regarding the state's finances:

- The gross state product ranks fifth among all states, with an estimated $528 billion in 2004. If Illinois were a country, it would rank 12th in the world in this department.

- The budget for the 2008 fiscal year is $50.7 billion.

- The median household income between 2004 and 2006 was $49,280.

- Nationally, Illinois ranks fifth in the number of women-owned firms, third in employment and fifth in sales.

- In 2006, the per capita income was $38,215, compared to the national $36,276.

- As of 2007, Illinois was home to 33 Fortune 500 companies.

Economic Innovators

Led by Milton Friedman and George Stigler (both Nobel laureates), the "Chicago school" was a loose term for a group of economists who gathered at the University of Chicago during the 1950s. The group embraced laissez-faire libertarianism in its methodology and is seen as being highly instrumental in the popularity of privatization, deregulation and other free-market ideologies around the world today. Friedman (1912–2006) taught at the university for 30 years and was called "the most influential economist of the second half of the 20th century" by *The Economist*. He received the Nobel Prize in Economics in

1976 for his "achievements in the fields of consumption analysis, monetary history and theory, and for his demonstration of the complexity of stabilization policy."

The leading Illinois companies (by revenue) as of 2007 are as follows:

Rank	Company	Revenue ($ millions)	City
1	Boeing	61,530.0	Chicago
2	State Farm Insurance	60,528.0	Bloomington
3	Sears Holdings	53,012.0	Hoffman Estates
4	Walgreen	47,409.0	Deerfield
5	Motorola	43,739.0	Schaumburg
6	Caterpillar	41,517.0	Peoria
7	Archer Daniels Midland	36,596.1	Decatur
8	Allstate	35,796.0	Northbrook
9	Deere & Co.	22,768.9	Moline
10	Abbott Laboratories	22, 476.3	Abbott Park
11	McDonald's	21,586.4	Oak Brook
12	UAL	19,340.0	Elk Grove Township
13	Sara Lee	18,539.0	Downers Grove
14	Exelon	15,654.0	Chicago
15	Illinois Tool Works	14,055.0	Glenview
16	Baxter International	10,378.0	Deerfield
17	Aon	10,311.0	Chicago
18	R.R. Donnelley & Sons	9316.6	Chicago
19	OfficeMax	8965.7	Naperville
20	Fortune Brands	8255.0	Deerfield

21	Smurfit-Stone Container	7944.0	Chicago
22	Integrys Energy Group	6979.2	Chicago
23	CDW	6785.5	Vernon Hills
24	Brunswick	5971.3	Lake Forest
25	Ryerson	5908.9	Chicago
26	W.W. Grainger	5883.7	Lake Forest
27	USG	5810.0	Chicago
28	Tribune	5582.6	Chicago
29	Anixter International	4938.6	Glenview
30	Wm. Wrigley Jr.	4686.0	Chicago
31	Tenneco	4685.0	Lake Forest
32	United Stationers	4546.9	Deerfield
33	Northern Trust Corp.	4473.0	Chicago

DID YOU  KNOW?

Scott Air Force Base operates out of St. Clair County and pumps as much as $2 billion into the area's economy each year.

Advanced Agriculture

Agriculture is big business in Illinois. It is the Midwest, after all—the climate is right, the soil is fertile, and there's fast and convenient transportation via air, water, roads and train. There are over 27 million acres of farmland in Illinois, and much of the state's income outside of the Chicagoland area comes from crops, especially corn and soybeans (two crops of which Illinois is consistently is one of the top producers). Other major agricultural outputs include wheat, dairy products, sorghum, hogs and cattle.

Soy What?

Soybeans are a very lucrative cash crop in Illinois—$3 billion annually!—and the international trading prices of this wonderful bean are set on the prices established in Decatur, a city aptly nicknamed the "Soybean Capital of the World." Soybeans are notoriously versatile and have a wide range of uses, including the production of flour, soap, crayons and biodiesel.

DID YOU KNOW?

Soybeans aren't a native U.S. crop—they were imported from China at the beginning of the 20th century. The rise of the soybean in the United States has been fast and furious: in 1914, for instance, only 1000 acres of soybeans were harvested. Today that figure has leaped to over 20 million acres.

Turning Corn into Cash

Illinois truly is corn country; one would be hard-pressed to find an area of the state where you won't see towering corn stalks planted in the fields along the sides of highways. And as a result of the growing demand for ethanol, corn production is on the rise throughout all of the United States, but especially so in Illinois. During the spring of 2007, Illinois farmers planted a record 12.9 million acres of corn—second only to Iowa.

Mason Money

Mason County is known as a leader in Illinois' agriculture industry, producing such diverse products as cucumbers, melons, tomatoes and popcorn. The county calls itself the "Imperial Valley of the Midwest."

Dear John

Moline, Illinois, is home to the corporate headquarters of Deere and Company, the world's leading manufacturer of farm and forestry equipment. In 1837, a man by the name of John Deere moved to Grand Detour and settled there with his family. Within a year, he had developed the world's first successful steel plow, using a broken, discarded saw blade. In 1848, he moved his company to Moline to take advantage of the transportation benefits afforded by its proximity to the Mississippi River. The company continued to grow throughout the 19th and 20th centuries, and today Deere and Company employ over 47,000 people in 27 countries, with a ranking of 98 in the Fortune 500.

Caterpillar

In 1925, the Holt Manufacturing Company and the C.L. Best Tractor Company (both based out of California) merged and became the Caterpillar Tractor Company. In the early 1930s, the company headquarters was moved to Peoria, where it remains today. Caterpillar Inc. is now the world's largest manufacturer of earth-moving machinery, supplying the construction, mining and forest industries with products such as tractors, trucks and excavators. They employ over 96,000 people worldwide, and the company's revenue in 2006 was over $40 billion.

In 2004, Caterpillar unwittingly found itself in the midst of some conflict related to the Middle East. The company had been selling bulldozers to the Israeli army, who were in turn using them to demolish homes of Palestinians in the West Bank and the Gaza Strip. The family of Rachel Corrie, an American woman who was killed in Gaza while trying to stop a Caterpillar bulldozer from destroying Palestinian property, sued the company in 2005, claiming that they knowingly committed war crimes by selling to the Israeli army. Spokespersons for Caterpillar said that they had "neither the legal right nor the means to police individual use of their equipment." A district judge in Washington, DC, dismissed the suit, but it caused some bad publicity for the company nonetheless.

Nuclear Powerhouse

The beginnings of nuclear industry go back to Illinois, when the Chicago Pile-1 (CP-1) was built at the University of Chicago under the supervision of Enrico Fermi, a prominent Italian physicist. The CP-1 was the world's first artificial nuclear reactor to produce a nuclear chain reaction. Today, there are six operating nuclear power plants in Illinois (in Braidwood, Byron, Dresden, LaSalle, Clinton and the Quad Cities), and as of 2005, the state ranked number one among the 31 states with nuclear capacity. Illinois has nearly as much nuclear capacity as the United Kingdom.

Some Coal Hard Facts

Coal mining is a big industry in Illinois; the state ranks ninth in the U.S. for overall production. Also...

☛ Illinois' coal reserves contain more British thermal units (BTUs) than the oil reserves of Saudi Arabia and Kuwait.

☛ Thirty-two million tons of coal were mined in Illinois in 2005.

☛ Coal is a $1 billion industry in Illinois (gross revenue).

☛ The average coal miner in Illinois earns a salary of $45,450.

☛ Coal underlies roughly 65 percent of Illinois' surface—37,000 square miles!

Techies Unite!

The state boasts over 2000 telecommunications establishments that employ over 50,000 workers, making it a leading base for this type of industry. High-tech firms employ 43 out of every 1000 private sector workers in Illinois. Greatly contributing to this are the educational institutions around the state. As of 2006, Illinois ranked sixth in the U.S. with 1199 science and engineering PhD degrees. These graduates joined the 25,320 science and engineering doctorates already working in the state.

COST OF LIVING

Prairie State Poverty

Illinois recently scored pretty poorly on a comprehensive examination of its poverty levels. As of 2006, over 1.5 million Illinoisans (out of 12 million) lived in poverty, and the state ranked last in the Midwest in the following categories:

- ☞ Overall poverty rate

- ☞ Child poverty rate

- ☞ Employment outlook (which was actually worst in the nation)

- ☞ Overall rate of uninsured people

- ☞ Homeownership rate

- ☞ Rate of children in households where the head of household did not finish high school

 The state has the 15th highest median annual income in the nation. Also, Illinois workers are well educated—56.2 percent boast an education beyond high school.

And some more slightly depressing facts about the state's economy:

- ☞ Illinois had the fourth-highest job growth rate in the nation from 2001 to 2004.

- ☞ Almost 25 percent of Illinois workers made less than $9.28 per hour in 2004.

- ☞ The rate of poverty increased in 31 counties between 2002 and 2003.

☛ The most poverty-stricken counties are Knox, Rock Island, Winnebago, Christian, Vermilion, St. Clair, Johnson and Pope.

☛ In 2004, women working full time had mean earnings of only 69 cents to every dollar earned by men working full time.

☛ From 1995 to 2005, the bankruptcy rate doubled.

☛ Illinois ranks second worst in the nation in small business ownership.

(*Source: Heartland Alliance Report on Illinois Poverty, 2006*)

It Ain't All Bad News

Three Illinois communities ranked in the top 20 among 141 housing markets nationwide in housing affordability during the fourth quarter of 2003: Springfield (5th), Peoria-Pekin (9th) and the Quad Cities (14th). Just so you know, housing affordability is determined by the relationship between median family income and median home prices.

Chicago Industry

Some info on the importance and general size of Chicago's economy:

☛ The Chicago area alone accounts for 4.1 percent of all retail sales in the United States. Such huge sales make Chicago the city with the third-largest revenue figures of all U.S. cities, and larger than 28 states in the Union.

☛ The Chicago area is home to two of the largest futures exchanges in the U.S., the Chicago Mercantile Exchange and the Chicago Board of Trade.

☞ Seventy-five nations maintain consulates in Illinois, and over 40 international banks have established branches or representative offices in Chicago.

☞ Chicago ranks second only to New York in the publishing industry.

Second Placers

Everyone knows Chicago is tops when it comes to cities in Illinois. But there *are* other cities—it's not just Chicago and a bunch of small towns. And so, a closer look at the economies of some second-tier cities:

	Elgin	Joliet	Peoria	Waukegan	Rockford	Aurora	Chicago
Population	116,349	154,231	135,639	103,291	191,211	170,684	2,873,790
Percent white	70.49%	69.32%	69.29%	50.14%	72.81%	68.07%	31.32%
Percent black	6.80%	18.16%	24.79%	19.21%	17.37%	11.06%	36.39%
Percent Hispanic	34.32%	18.41%	2.51%	44.82%	10.18%	32.56%	26.02%
Median household income	$59,771	$50,725	$41,782	$46,868	$44,820	$59,919	$46,748
Median home price	$187,290	$136,834	$96,486	$147,928	$93,645	$171,683	$254,500
Home price gain (2–5 years)	13.67%	10.16%	7.84%	9.39%	7.32%	7.10%	12.6%
Air pollution index*	55	57	NA	37	70	95	38.1
Personal crime risk*	72	126	174	86	140	81	358
Property crime risk*	52	128	169	125	155	52	173

*lower number is better
(*Sources: http://www.cnnmoney.com; homeinsight.com; Onboard LLC; U.S. Census 2000.*)

FAMOUS ILLINOIS MERCHANTS

The Grand Marshall

Marshall Field (1834–1906) established the first modern department store in 1881. Field's commitment to customer service became the standard business model for retail and is best illustrated in two famous quotes frequently attributed to him—"Give the lady what she wants," and "The customer is always right." In 2006, much to the distaste of many longtime Chicago loyalists, the retail juggernaut Macy's bought out this beloved Chicago institution.

Ward on the Street

Aaron Montgomery Ward had a brilliant idea: why not let people shop by mail? And so in 1872, he started the first mail-order business in the U. S., the Montgomery Ward & Company of Chicago. Customers could leaf through the pages of furniture, clothes and appliances to find what they wanted and have it delivered to their house. The catalog was especially popular with rural types who lived many miles from stores. Montgomery Ward enjoyed great success in the 1800s and 1900s before going out of business in 2001.

Sears Towering

Richard Sears and Alvah Roebuck started their own mail-order catalog in 1893. Originally, Sears was selling watches on mail-order, but Sears, Roebuck and Company eventually became known as a place to buy *everything*—from groceries to bicycles. In 1925, Sears opened their first retail store in Chicago; by the time World War II broke out, it had over 600 retail outlets in operation, and the company was the largest retailer in the U.S. until the early 1980s. They merged with Kmart in 2005.

Drugstore Pioneer

In 1901, Charles C. Walgreen opened the first of many drugstores on the south side of Chicago. Walgreen's store sold hot sandwiches and malt milkshakes (which Walgreen's employee Ivar "Pop" Coulson is credited with inventing), giving the store a more community feel. It's said that when folks called in an order, Walgreen repeated the order loudly enough so that one of his assistants could quickly prepare the order and deliver it to the customer. Walgreen would prolong the conversation so that the order could arrive at the caller's door while he or she was still talking on the phone—pretty impressive!

In 1997, Walgreens was the first drugstore to open a drive-thru window for customers to pick up their prescriptions. Today, Walgreens is a rapidly growing chain with 6000 locations in the U.S. and Puerto Rico, filling one million prescriptions a day. It's headquartered in Deerfield.

GETTING FROM HERE TO THERE

O'Hare, Oh My

O'Hare International Airport in Chicago handled 931,000 flights in 2003, making it the world's busiest airport. Today it is the second busiest in terms of traffic, behind Hartsfield-Jackson Atlanta International Airport. It also ranked second in the world in 2006 in total passengers, with 76,248,911. From 2004 to 2006, O'Hare has been awarded the honor of Best Airport in North America by *Global Traveler* magazine, and from 1998 through 2003, it received the same distinction from *Business Traveler* magazine. O'Hare isn't perfect, though: the airport is responsible for one sixth of the United States' flight cancellations. O'Hare's abbreviation is "ORD," which is a little confusing: the letters are meant to stand for Orchard Field, the original name of the airport. The name was changed in 1949, in honor of Edward H. "Butch" O'Hare, a naval pilot who died during a World War II mission in the South Pacific.

Trains Aplenty

Illinois is the center of the nation's railroads, and Chicago is the largest rail gateway. In all, 52 railroads are able to provide service from Illinois to every part of the U.S. The metropolitan area of Chicago itself is served by the Regional Transit Authority (RTA), which is in charge of all public transportation, including the Chicago Transit Authority (CTA), which operates buses and trains within the city; Metra, a train service that connects Chicago with its many suburbs) and Pace, which provides bus service throughout the city's suburbs.

The "L"

Chicago is famous for its system of elevated trains, which is colloquially referred to as the "L" or the "El." It consists of eight rapid transit lines spanning over 222 miles throughout the city and its closest suburbs and is the third-busiest rapid transit system in the United States, behind only New York and Washington, DC. But allow us to "El-aborate" a little more on these fine lines.

☞ Each of the eight lines is named after a color: the Red Line, Blue Line, Brown Line, Green Line, Pink Line, Orange Line, Purple Line and Yellow Line.

☞ The Red Line and the Blue Line are the only two lines that run 24 hours a day, and the Red is the busiest of the lines.

☞ Roughly 15 percent of the "L" tracks run in underground subways—which is really the opposite of "elevated." Oh well.

☞ The oldest tracks date back to 1892, making the "L" line the third-oldest rapid transit system in North America after New York and Boston.

☞ The "L" had an annual ridership of 195.2 million in 2006, the highest since 1993.

☞ 658,524 people ride the "L" each weekday.

☞ The CTA, which runs the "L," employs over 11,000 people.

Midway

Midway International Airport used to be top dog not only in Chicago and Illinois but also in the U.S. and worldwide. Shortly after opening in 1928, Midway became the world's busiest airport, and it held onto that title until the 1960s, when O'Hare dominated Chicago air travel. Originally called Chicago Municipal Airport, its name was changed to "Midway" in 1949, after the historic Battle of Midway in World War II. In 2007, Midway ranked number three in the U.S. in on-time arrivals.

 Chicago's airports generate $45 billion annually and create over 540,000 jobs in the region.

Major Highways

☛ One of the biggest highways in Illinois is Interstate 55, which runs north-south from downtown Chicago all the way down to East St. Louis and passes through the cities of Springfield and Bloomington. The interstate logs a distance of 294 Illinois miles and follows quite closely the route of the famous Route 66, which was decommissioned in 1985. In Chicago, I-55 is known as the Adlai Stevenson Expressway ("Stevenson" for short, named after a former governor of Illinois).

☛ The east-west Interstate 74 runs across the northern part of Illinois, starting near the Quad Cities and leaving the state just east of Danville, for a total of 220 state miles. It traverses the major cities of Rock Island, Peoria, Bloomington and Champaign-Urbana.

DID YOU KNOW?

Illinois boasts the largest number of personalized license plates of any state.

STATE OF HEALTH

The Bad News...

Illinois is doing well in some areas of public health, but in others...not so much. Let's have a look at the areas in which the state is doing well and which areas need a little improvement. We'll give you the bad news first:

- Life expectancy in Illinois is 76.4 years as of 2006, which ranks below average as the 33rd overall state.

- Illinois had 1011 suicides on record in 2004, eighth highest in the United States. Illinois males are seven times more likely to commit suicide than Illinois females.

☛ 23.9 percent of Illinois adults in 2006 were medically obese, making it the 23rd-heaviest state in the U.S. The state also had the seventh-highest overweight levels for low-income children ages two through five, at 14 percent.

☛ Illinois has the seventh-highest number of AIDS cases in the United States since 1981—32,685 as of 2005.

…And the Good News

☛ According to the United Health Foundation's 2006 edition of "America's Health Rankings," Illinois is exactly average—it was ranked 25 out of the 50 states. More encouraging, perhaps, is that Illinois was the most improved state between the 2005 and 2006 editions: smoking declined from 22.2 percent to 19.9 percent of the population, child poverty declined from 18 percent to 15.6 percent, and the infant mortality rate declined from 7.2 to 7.0 deaths per every 1000 live births.

☛ The University of Chicago Medical Center was named to *U.S. News and World Report*'s prestigious Honor Roll in 2007—the hospital was one of only 18 in the nation to make the list, and the only one to ever make it from the state of Illinois.

☛ Trust for America's Health (TFAH), a "non-profit, non-partisan organization dedicated to saving lives by protecting the health of every community and working to make disease prevention a national priority," commended Illinois in 2004 for cancer tracking. The state received an "A" for maintaining high-quality cancer data and for having one of the nation's best cancer registry programs.

Home to the AMA

Since 1902, the American Medical Association has been head-quartered in Chicago. The AMA is the largest association of med students and doctors in the United States, and its journal, the *Journal of the American Medical Association*, is the largest weekly medical journal in the world. Its mission is to promote the art and science of medicine and the betterment of public health, and it functions by uniting physicians so that they can work on the many public health issues facing the United States today.

A Cure for Diabetes?

Since 2004, Jose Oberholzer, director of cell and pancreas transplantation at the University of Illinois Medical Center at Chicago, has been leading the Chicago Project—an effort to cure diabetes by producing islet cells from donor pancreases that can be transplanted into patients. Oberholzer leads a team of 15 physicians and scientists from Canada, France and Israel, and since 2005, they have successfully transplanted islet cells into eight patients.

The Bionic Woman

A former U.S. marine named Claudia Mitchell lost her left arm in a motorcycle accident in 2004. In September 2006, the Rehabilitation Institute of Chicago unveiled a truly inspiring accomplishment: they were able to give Mitchell a functioning bionic arm. Doctors removed the nerve endings that once controlled her arm from her shoulder and rerouted and connected those nerves to her chest muscle. Mitchell can now control the movements of her arm the way most people can: simply by thinking about it. Furthermore, it's hoped that this technology will be able to help the many members of the military who have lost limbs during the recent wars in Iraq and Afghanistan.

Universal Health Care

In 2005, Governor Rod Blagojevich signed into law the All Kids health insurance bill, which obligates Illinois to provide "affordable, comprehensive health insurance" to every child in the state. In March 2007, he proposed a substantial tax increase ($7.6 billion) that would pay for universal healthcare in Illinois by taxing large Illinois businesses. It was defeated by a vote of 107–0. And so the healthcare fight in America continues...

ILLINOIS INSIDER Governor Blagojevich has taken a hard stance on the "morning-after pill." In 2005, he issued an emergency order whereby pharmacists had to fill all contraceptive prescriptions regardless of their own personal religious or ethical beliefs. As of 2006, all pharmacies have to post signs on their premises that outline women's rights to contraceptives. Famous Christian evangelist Pat Robertson filed a lawsuit against Blagojevich on behalf of five pharmacists who were suspended by Walgreens for refusing to dispense the drug.

HIGHER LEARNING

Fast Facts on Illinois Intellectuals

There are 69 universities in the state of Illinois, and the first college in the state to conduct classes and grant a baccalaureate degree was Illinois College, founded in 1829. (William Jenning Bryan, a congressman, secretary of state and three-time presidential nominee, was an alumnus—class of 1881.) Here's some info on some other prominent Illinois universities:

☛ Columbia College Chicago: founded in 1890, in Chicago. It's the largest arts and media college in the nation.

☛ DePaul University: founded in 1898, in Chicago. With a student population of over 24,000 students, DePaul is the nation's largest Catholic university, and in 2007, the *Princeton Review* declared the school number one in the nation in the "Diverse Student Population" category.

☛ Lewis University: founded in 1932, in Romeoville.

☛ Loyola University Chicago: founded in 1870, in Chicago.

☛ Northern Illinois University: founded in 1895, in DeKalb.

☛ Northwestern University: founded in 1851, in Evanston. *U.S. News and World Report* ranks it 14th in its survey of all American universities.

☛ Southern Illinois University: founded in 1869, in Carbondale.

☛ Quincy University: founded in 1860, in Quincy.

☛ University of Chicago: founded in 1890 by richest-guy-in-American-history John D. Rockefeller, this university is one of the most prestigious academic institutions in America. It's also home to the largest university press in the United States, which publishes the highly influential *Chicago Manual of Style.*

☛ University of Illinois: founded in 1867, in Urbana. It consists of three campuses: Urbana-Champaign, Chicago and Springfield. Urbana-Champaign (commonly referred to as "U of I") is the largest and most prestigious of the three universities. Its library is the largest public academic library in the nation and contains over 10 million volumes of work.

☛ Western Illinois University: founded in 1899, in Macomb.

More on the U of I System

☛ *U.S. News and World Report* ranked the graduate and undergraduate accounting programs at U of I as number one in the U.S. in 2006. And the school's graduate engineering program was ranked as the fourth best nationally.

☛ It's estimated that one in ten Chicagoans with a college degree graduated from the University of Illinois-Chicago (UIC).

☛ The University of Illinois College of Medicine is the nation's largest medical school, with over 2600 students on campuses in Chicago, Urbana, Peoria and Rockford.

☛ Go Greek! U of I is home to the largest Greek system in the world, with 60 fraternities and 36 sororities; 22 percent of all undergraduates are involved in Greek life.

☛ With 42,728 students as of the summer of 2007, U of I is one of the 20-largest universities in the United States.

☛ The university has an annual budget of over $1 billion!

The mascot of Southern Illinois University in Carbondale is the saluki, a breed of dog that originated in the Middle East. Also, one of the Amtrak trains serving the state of Illinois is called the "Saluki."

Class Clowns

Students at Illinois State University (ISU) in Normal can earn class credit by learning fire-breathing, juggling and unicycling. How? Because ISU is home to Gamma Phi Circus, the nation's oldest collegiate circus. In 1926, Clifford "Pop" Horton, a gymnastics instructor at ISU, organized a group of students to do pyramids and tumbles at the school's sporting events, which led to the formation of the Gamma Phi fraternity in 1929. Two years later, the fraternity held its first circus performance, and in 1938, women were allowed into the group. The name was then changed to Gamma Phi Circus, and residents of Normal-Bloomington have had their own personal circus entertainment ever since.

DID YOU  KNOW?

ISU is also home to the one of the world's largest residence halls. The 28 floors (298 feet) of Watterson Towers house 2200 students in all!

Get Your ACT Together!

Illinois ACT scores improved in 2007 to an average composite score of 20.5, up from 20.1 in 2002. However, the state scores below the national average in all four testing areas (math, science, English and reading) as well as the national composite average of 21.2. It could be argued that these results are somewhat skewed, though, as Illinois, along with Colorado and Michigan, are the only states in the union that require every public high school graduate to take the test (in the other 47 states, only students that intend to enroll in college must take the test). Another bit of ACT trivia: in 2007, 68 Illinois students (out of approximately 140,000 test takers) scored a perfect 36.

On the SAT—a competitor of the ACT and the most popular college entrance exam nationally—Illinois students bested the national average, though only 11,000 high school students in the state took it.

What Else?

More education odds and ends:

☞ Illinois has the 14th best pupil/teacher ratio in the nation, with 16.5 teachers to every student.

☞ The state has 59,537 people with a postsecondary degree—sixth highest in the nation.

☞ 81 percent of Illinoisans over the age of 25 have a high school degree, and 27 percent over the age of 25 have a bachelor's degree or higher. Both statistics place Illinois as better than the national average.

☞ The Chicago Public Library has 79 branches, making it one of the largest urban library systems in the world. Also, when the Harold Washington Library Center opened to the Chicago public in 1991, it was the largest public library in the world.

BY THE PEOPLE, FOR THE PEOPLE

Illinois is the home of many important and popular politicians, movers and shakers who have greatly influenced our American lives. Long a state that was politically up-for-grabs, Illinois has gradually become a reliably Democratic state—citizens have voted for Democratic nominees in the past four presidential elections, going back to 1992. Republicans still generally win out in rural areas and small cities, but Chicago and other large cities make Illinois the most stable Democratic state in the Midwest. As of 2007, both Illinois senators were Democrats, as were the state governor and the mayor of Chicago.

Corruption with a Capital "C"

Chicago politics have a tendency to be a little shady, and the history of Chicago has largely been shaped by Democratic "machine" politics. To live in the city is to accept that corruption plays a major role in how things get done around town—that's just the way things have been since the days of Al Capone (and even well before that). And in the world of city politics, the Democrats reign supreme: mayoral elections are often won during the Democratic primaries, as Republicans typically stand little chance of getting elected in the city (it hasn't happened since 1927).

Boss Man

Richard J. Daley (1902–76) served as mayor of Chicago during some of the most formative years of the city's history, from 1955 until his death. "Boss" Daley was notorious for his method of city machine politics (read: widespread corruption) as well as for

revitalizing Chicago's downtown Loop area and for keeping Chicago from becoming, as journalist Elizabeth Taylor put it, "another Detroit or Cleveland"—Midwestern rust belt cities that trail Chicago in terms of financial success and cultural output. Interestingly, Daley—a lifelong Democrat—was first elected to office as a Republican. When a Republican candidate for the state legislature died during his campaign in 1936, Daley joined the race, taking the open spot on the ballot (two Democrats from Daley's district were already on the ballot, which prevented him from running as a Dem). Once elected, though, he immediately joined the House Democratic Caucus and never looked back.

Three Chicago Firsts

☛ Harold Washington (1922–87) was the first black mayor of Chicago, serving the city from 1983 until his death. Twice elected, Washington was a World War II veteran and a graduate of Northwestern University's School of Law (he was a practicing attorney for 13 years before entering politics). He died of a massive heart attack at his desk in city hall.

☛ Jane Byrne (born May 24, 1934) was the first female mayor of Chicago, elected in 1979. Her victory in the Democratic primary over then-mayor Michael Bilandic (a man largely seen as embodying the status quo of Chicago machine politics) is considered one of the biggest political upsets in Illinois history. Byrne went on to win 82 percent of the vote in the general election, sweeping all 50 of the city's wards. Her reign as mayor lasted until 1983, when she was defeated in the Democratic primary by Washington. (Future mayor Richard M. Daley also ran in this primary, which split the white vote, resulting in Washington's nomination and election.)

☛ In 2003, Tom Tunney (born August 22, 1955, in Chicago) was officially elected alderman of the 44th ward of Chicago, which includes Wrigley Field and the Boystown neighborhood. Tunney is the first openly gay alderman in the city's history.

For the Women

Illinois has a rich history of embracing the women's movement. In 1920, it was the first state in the union to ratify the 19th Amendment, which gave women the right to vote. In 1978, Hannah Gray became the president of the prestigious University of Chicago, making her the first woman president of a major American university. And in 1992, Carol Moseley-Braun was elected to the U.S. Senate. She was the first (and to this day, the only) African American woman elected to the office.

YOU ARE NOW OFFICIALLY A WOMAN PERSON

WOMAN PERSON

DID YOU KNOW?

The first African American to vote (following the passage of the 15th Amendment) was David Strother, who did so on April 4, 1870, in El Paso, Illinois.

The New Mayor Daley

Chicago just can't get enough of their Daleys. Richard M. Daley (born April 24, 1942) is the oldest son of legendary Chicago mayor Richard J. Daley and is on course to become a legendary Chicago figure in his own right. He's served as the boss of the city since 1989 and is poised to break his father's record of longest-serving mayor of Chicago if he completes his current term. Daley is a Democrat like his father and is a vocal supporter of gun control, gay rights and environmental awareness. A wildly popular mayor with clout and influence to spare, Daley was re-elected in 2007 with over 70 percent of the city's vote. In 2005, *Time* magazine selected him as the best big-city mayor in America.

Governor's Blues

Before Republican George Ryan was elected governor in 1999, he had served as secretary of state for Illinois for eight years, and it was those years that ended his long career in Illinois politics. In 1994, a truck accident in Wisconsin killed six children, and a subsequent investigation revealed a system in place within Ryan's office wherein unskilled drivers could acquire truck driver's licenses through bribes. The scandal slowly gained momentum and intensified when Ryan was elected governor. Eventually, the investigation found evidence of illegal contracts, kickbacks and misuse of government money—all under Ryan's watch. Facing possible charges, Ryan declared that he would not seek another term as governor in 2002. The following year, he was indicted on federal charges of fraud, conspiracy and racketeering, and in 2006 he was convicted of 18 of those charges. He stands to serve six and a half years in prison, though his lawyers have appealed the sentence. Ryan did get one major thing done before leaving Springfield: a vocal opponent of the death penalty, he commuted the sentences of all 167 Illinois inmates on death row (they were all reduced to life sentences).

The Mighty Guv'nor Thompson

The longest-serving governor of Illinois was Republican James R. Thompson (born May 8, 1936, in Chicago), who held the office from 1977 all the way to 1991. Thompson received his law degree from Northwestern University (where he later taught) and served as U.S. Attorney for the Northern District of Illinois, where he established a reputation of prosecuting corrupt (and usually Democratic) public figures, many of whom worked for the first Mayor Daley. In 1993, the State of Illinois Center in downtown Chicago was renamed the James R. Thompson Center in honor of him. Thompson appeared in the news again in 2003, when he served on the 9/11 Commission.

Local Boy Makes Good

Dennis Hastert is a tried-and-true Prairie Stater. Born in Aurora (January 2, 1942) and raised in Oswego, Hastert graduated from Wheaton College and earned his master's degree in education from Northern Illinois University. He then moved to Yorkville, where he taught history and government to high school students. In 1980, he was elected to the Illinois House of Representatives, where he served three terms. In 1986, he ran for and was elected to Congress, as the representative of Illinois' 14th congressional district. When the Republicans took control of the House in 1995, Hastert was named Chief Deputy Whip, and when Newt Gingrich stepped down as Speaker of the House in 1998, Hastert was chosen to fill his shoes. Shortly after being re-elected to office in 2006, Hastert announced plans to retire from Congress at the end of his 11th term.

In June 2006, Hastert became the longest-serving Republican Speaker of the House in U.S. history, breaking the previous record set by Joseph Gurney Cannon. Cannon, by the way, was an Illinois congressman who was featured on the first issue of *Time* magazine ever published, on March 3, 1923.

Rahm-Bo

Rahm Emanuel (born November 29, 1959, in Chicago) is a DC power player in every sense of the word—and success seems to follow him everywhere he goes. His first high-profile gig was as senior adviser and chief fundraiser for Richard M. Daley's run for mayor of Chicago in 1989. From there, he went on to work for Bill Clinton's presidential primary campaign in 1991, where he was director of finance. When Clinton was elected, Emanuel was appointed senior advisor to the President for policy and strategy. In 2002, he ran for the U.S. House seat in the fifth district of Illinois (a vacant seat due to its former occupant, Rod Blagojevich, successfully running for governor that year) and was elected; he's since been re-elected twice, and in 2005 he was named chair of the Democratic Congressional Campaign Committee. Rahm's also a pretty unique character. Here's a little more about this Illinois congressman.

☛ An often-told story around Washington is that Emanuel once mailed a two-and-a-half-foot dead fish to a former co-worker after they parted ways.

☛ His colleagues have dubbed him "Rahmbo," because of his intense nature.

☛ Emanuel lost half of his right middle finger to a meat slicer when he was a teenager.

☛ The character of Josh Lyman (played by actor Bradley Whitford) on the popular TV series *The West Wing* is said to be based on Emanuel.

☛ Rahm's brother Ari is a successful talent agent in Hollywood, representing stars such as Larry David, Mark Wahlberg and Michael Moore. Also, like his brother, Ari has a fictional entertainment figure based on his life: the character of Ari Gold (played by Jeremy Piven) on the hit HBO series *Entourage* is based on Ari Emanuel. And Piven himself is a Chicagoan. It all comes back to Illinois!

☛ Emanuel is a trained ballet dancer and was even awarded a college scholarship for ballet, though he turned it down.

PRESIDENTIAL PROWESS

The Gipper

Ronald Reagan was born in Tampico on February 6, 1911, but he spent his youth in Dixon. He went to Eureka College and became a radio broadcaster, often working Chicago Cubs baseball games. He later moved to California to pursue work as a film actor, starring in such films as *Kings Row* and *Knute Rockne, All American*, where he played the role of George "the Gipper" Gipp, a nickname that stuck with him for the rest of his life. He became governor of California in 1966 and reigned as president of the United States from 1981 to 1989. Diagnosed with Alzheimer's disease in 1994, he died in 2004 at the age of 93.

Honest Abe

What is there to say about Abraham Lincoln (1809–65) that hasn't already been said? Well, for one, he was not actually born in the Land of Lincoln—he grew up in Kentucky and then Indiana before his family moved to Illinois' Macon County in 1830. But Illinois is where Lincoln began his political career in 1832, and it's likely the state that remembers him most fondly. Although every state celebrates his birthday on Presidents' Day, Illinois observes it as a separate legal holiday, called Lincoln's Birthday, celebrated every February 12. In case you didn't already know, Lincoln served as the 16th president of the United States from 1861 until his assassination in 1865. If you want to know what he looked like, just pick up a five dollar bill, or—if times are tough financially—a penny. His bearded face graces both units of currency.

In April 2005, the Abraham Lincoln Presidential Library and Museum opened in Springfield. It's been the most-visited presidential museum in North America since its opening.

DID YOU KNOW?

Reagan ranked second in a Gallup poll taken in February 2007 that asked respondents to name the greatest president in U.S. history. Who came in first? Another president with strong Illinois roots: Abraham Lincoln.

Obama-Rama

If such a thing exists as a rock star in this 21st century political climate, few would argue that Barack Obama is that man. At the 2004 Democratic National Convention, Obama, a relatively unknown junior senator from Illinois at the time, gave a rousing

speech that has essentially catapulted him to political stardom. Obama's life story is the picture of diversity: born in 1961 in Hawaii to a white Kansan woman and a Kenyan father, Obama also lived in Jakarta as a child. He was later the president of the Harvard Law Review (the most respected legal review in the United States—no small feat) before moving to Chicago to teach at the University of Chicago and do community organization work on the city's south side. Obama is now a candidate for president of the United States; whether or not he's elected in 2008, it seems certain that he'll remain a charismatic and influential figure in American politics for years to come.

Hillary Rodham Clinton

Standing in Obama's way for the Democratic nomination for president in 2008 is none other than Hillary Rodham Clinton, wife of former president Bill Clinton, and herself an Illinois native. Hillary Rodham was born at Edgewater Hospital in Chicago on October 26, 1947, and was raised in Park Ridge, a suburb of the city. Her father, Hugh, made his living in textiles in Chicago, where he worked at the Merchandise Mart and later at a fabric printing plant he opened on the north side of the city.

A graduate of Wellesley College and Yale Law School, Hillary married Bill Clinton in 1975 and became First Lady of Arkansas in 1979, a title she held for a total of 12 years. In 1992, she became a different kind of First Lady—as in the First Lady of the United States—when her husband was elected president. That role was apparently not enough for her, though, and in 2000 she was elected senator for the state of New York—becoming the first First Lady to be elected to public office as well as the first female senator for New York.

MUSIC

Louis Louis!

Illinois was a popular destination for many black musicians during the Great Migration from the South in the early 1900s, and the 1920s in Chicago are often considered the golden age of jazz. Louis Armstrong (1901–71) has a lot to do with this perception. He was born in New Orleans (the city's airport is now named after him) but migrated to Chicago in the 1920s.

"Satchmo," as he was called, made his name trumpeting for bands such as the Hot Fives and the Hot Sevens. Later in his career, he became famous for his unique voice, and he is often credited with the popularization of scat singing (think "dippity-doo-dop-ba-bop-bop-boom").

Jumpin' Jazz!

Illinois was the breeding ground for some of the most influential names in the history of one of America's prized cultural exports—jazz music.

Miles Ahead of the Pack

Miles Davis (1926–91) was born in Alton and lived for a time in East St. Louis. A talented composer and trumpeter, Davis was a consistently innovative figure in modern jazz and was instrumental in the development of its many iterations, such as bebop, cool jazz and jazz-rock fusion. He's considered by many to be the greatest jazz musician of all time.

The King of Swing

Benny Goodman (1909–86), a.k.a. the King of Swing, was a world-famous clarinet player born in Chicago. Credited with ushering in the swing era of jazz, Goodman also forged the way for the racial integration of jazz—he was one of the few white musicians (if not *the* first) to regularly record and perform with black musicians in the 1930s. His band was the first jazz band to play Carnegie Hall, in 1938, and he has honorary doctorates in music from Harvard, Yale, Columbia and, of course, the University of Illinois.

A Little Bit Country

Mercer County is proud to call Susy Bogguss one of its own. The acclaimed country music singer made her mark in the 1980s but took a break during the mid-1990s to begin a family. Today, although she's yet to reclaim her chart-topping popularity, she maintains a strong following, which includes the county's residents among her most loyal fans, thank you very much!

City Folks

No discussion of Illinois music would be complete without talking about the group of musicians who decided to name their band after the largest city in the state. The band Chicago formed in 1967 at DePaul University; they were originally called The Big Thing, and later, Chicago Transit Authority, which was also the name of their debut album. (The real Chicago Transit Authority, the one that makes sure the trains and buses in the city run on time, threatened legal action against the group shortly after they released the album, and the band shortened the name to Chicago.) Some say the band is cheesy, but you can't argue with the group's stats:

☞ 120 million records sold worldwide

☞ 18 gold albums, 13 platinum albums, and five that have hit number one on the U.S. charts

☞ Five gold singles

☞ A Grammy for Best Performance by a Duo or Group in 1977

And believe it or not, the band Chicago is one of the most successful American pop groups of the 20th century. Take that, Boston (the group)!

Cheap Trick

Cheap Trick came out of Rockford in the late 1970s and is maybe best known for their hit single, "I Want You to Want Me." They continue to have a cult following, and the band is responsible for some music you're probably familiar with but don't know about. For one, they wrote and performed the theme song to *The Colbert Report*, the hit show on Comedy Central. They're the performers of the theme song to *That '70s Show*, though they didn't write it (the song is called "In the Street" and was written by the band Big Star). In 2007, a resolution was passed in the Illinois state senate proclaiming April 1 of every year as Cheap Trick Day in the State of Illinois.

Uncle Tupelo/Son Volt/Wilco

In 1987, Belleville, Illinois residents Jay Farrar, Jeff Tweedy and Mike Heidorn formed Uncle Tupelo, a country band with heavy punk rock influences. They only released four albums before breaking up in 1994 but are considered by many to be the pioneers of a genre of music called alternative country. Their influence was important enough to inspire a magazine, *No Depression*—named after the band's first album—devoted to covering the genre. After their acrimonious split, Farrar formed Son Volt, a popular Americana group that relies heavily on the rootsy Uncle Tupelo sound. Tweedy picked up and moved to Chicago, where he formed Wilco, a experimental rock band that has developed a reputation for consistently exploring new musical territory with each album. Wilco won a Grammy for Best Alternative Music Album in 2005 for their sixth studio release, *A Ghost Is Born*. The group's latest album, *Sky Blue Sky*, debuted at number four on the U.S. Billboard 200 charts, selling 87,000 copies its first week.

Traveling Troubadour

In 2005, indie-rock singer-songwriter Sufjan Stevens released the album *Illinois*, the second installment in his pledge to make an album about each one of the 50 U.S. states. (His first was an ode to his home state of Michigan.) The album, which features songs about John Wayne Gacy, Casimir Pulaski Day, Jelly Roll Morton and other assorted bits of Illinois trivia, topped many music critics' year-end lists. It also won the Pantheon Prize, which is awarded to the best album of the year that doesn't achieve "gold" status (sales over 500,000 copies). Clever titles from the album (and there are almost too many to note) include "The Seer's Tower" and "Come On! Feel the Illinoise!"

In 1999, the Rolling Stones played a surprise concert at the Double Door, a small venue in the Wicker Park neighborhood of Chicago that holds only 473 people. Quite a step down from the football stadiums Mick and Keith usually play!

The Smashing Pumpkins

The most successful band to emerge out of Illinois in the 1990s was the Smashing Pumpkins, an alt-rock group led by the famously bald Billy Corgan. Formed in Chicago in 1988, the Pumpkins hit it big in 1993 with their album *Siamese Dream*. They followed up that success in 1995 with a double album, *Mellon Collie and the Infinite Sadness*, which debuted at number one on the *Billboard* charts and was certified platinum nine times in the U.S. The usual suspects of drugs and inner turmoil caused the band to break up in 2000, when they played a farewell show at the Metro club in Chicago. As of 2007, the Smashing Pumpkins are touring again, albeit without two of the original members.

A Pretty Successful Dropout

Born in Atlanta on June 8, 1977, Kanye West moved to Chicago when he was three years old and was raised on the south side of the city, attending high school in the suburb of Oak Lawn. His mother, Donda West, worked in the English department at Chicago State University, which is interesting when you consider that all of West's albums so far—*College Dropout*, *Late Registration* and *Graduation*—deal with educational experiences. Unfortunately, in a rather shocking turn of events, Donda died from complications related to cosmetic surgery on November 10, 2007. Today, of course, Kanye is one of hip-hop's brightest stars, but he cut his teeth producing hit singles for artists such as Jay-Z, Alicia Keys and Ludacris. Kanye's a talented fella, but he's also got quite the ego, and he loves to court controversy. A few of his not-so-subtle moments:

☞ In 2006, he appeared on the cover of *Rolling Stone* wearing a crown of thorns on his dome, in an obvious comparison to Jesus Christ.

☞ He once claimed that he would be in the Bible if it were written in the present day.

☞ During a televised concert benefit for the victims of Hurricane Katrina, he decided not to read his cue card and said off-the-cuff, very matter-of-factly to the entire national NBC audience that "George [W.] Bush doesn't care about black people."

☞ After losing all five awards that he was nominated for at the MTV Video Music Awards ceremony in 2007, West threw a temper tantrum backstage, claiming that he would never return to MTV again. (Um, Kanye? Those awards are meaningless.)

☞ The temper tantrum at MTV wasn't exactly unprecedented. After the video for his song "Touch the Sky" lost out to Justice and Simian's "We Are Your Friends" at the 2006 MTV Europe VMAs, West stormed the stage, grabbed the microphone and declared himself to be the rightful winner. "It cost a million dollars, Pamela Anderson was in it. I jumped across canyons," were the reasons he gave for why he deserved the prize. He also claimed, "If I don't win, the awards show loses credibility." Seriously. We can't make this stuff up.

Chicago is generally given credit for being the place where house music was invented. In fact, it's widely believed that the term "house music" was derived from the Warehouse, a nightclub in the city where legendary DJ Frankie Knuckles used to spin records. For those not hip to the club culture, "house music" is basically disco-influenced electronic dance music.

Famous Musicians Born in Illinois

☛ Common, rapper (born Lonnie Rashid Lynn Jr. on March 13, 1972, in Chicago)

☛ Billy Corgan, lead singer of the Smashing Pumpkins (March 17, 1967, in Elk Grove Village)

☛ Dan Fogelberg, '70s singer/songwriter (August 13, 1951, in Peoria)

☛ Herbie Hancock, jazz musician (April 12, 1940, in Chicago)

☛ Burl Ives, folk singer and Academy Award winner (June 14, 1909, in Hunt)

☛ R. Kelly, rapper (born Robert Sylvester Kelly on January 8, 1967, in Chicago)

☛ Allison Krauss, bluegrass artist (July 23, 1971, in Decatur)

☛ Ludacris, rapper (September 11, 1977, in Champaign)

☛ John Prine, folk singer/country songwriter (October 10, 1946, in Maywood)

☛ Twista, rapper (born Carl Terrell Mitchell on November 27, 1973, in Chicago)

☛ Eddie Vedder, lead singer of Pearl Jam (December 23, 1964, in Evanston)

☛ Pete Wentz, bassist/songwriter for Fall Out Boy (June 5, 1979, in Wilmette)

☛ Michelle Williams, singer for Destiny's Child (July 23, 1980, in Rockford)

☛ Gretchen Wilson, country singer (June 26, 1973, in Pocahontas)

LITERATURE

Illinois—especially Chicago—has an especially rich literary tradition, producing and nourishing some of the most respected and successful writers of the 20th century.

When Papa Was Just a Boy

Ernest Hemingway (1899–1961) was born in what is now Oak Park, a Chicago suburb then known as Cicero. He spent his childhood in Illinois before going overseas to fight in World War I. He returned after the war and lived for a time on the north side of Chicago, where he married his first wife, Hadley. Hemingway went on to write several novels that are now part of the American canon, including *The Sun Also Rises*, *A Farewell to Arms* and *The Old Man and the Sea*, for which he won the Pulitzer Prize in 1953. A consummate outdoorsman and worldly traveler, Hemingway won the Nobel Prize for Literature in 1954.

Hipster Hero

A Michigan transplant, Nelson Algren (1910–88) moved to Chicago as a child and was immediately fascinated by the mean streets of the city. In 1950, he won the National Book Award for his novel *The Man with the Golden Arm*, a story about back-alley drunks, drug addicts, fighters and gamblers on the west side of Chicago. He followed this up with *Chicago: City on the Make*, a long-form essay about his beloved city, about which he said, "You'll never love another. Like loving a woman with a broken nose, you may well find lovelier lovelies. But never a lovely so real." Algren has become something of a cult author, beloved by modern hipsters who romanticize his cityscape descriptions and vice-addled, down-on-their-luck protagonists.

Giver of Nicknames

Galesburg native Carl Sandburg (1878–1967) won two Pulitzer Prizes—one in 1951 for a collection of poems, and one in 1940 for a biography of Abraham Lincoln. Sandburg lived in Chicago from 1912 to 1928, and much of his finest poetry features the city as a backdrop. Sandburg's poetry is responsible for not just one, but two of Chicago's nicknames (and unique ones at that): "Hog Butcher to the World" and "The City of Big Shoulders."

Look Out Bellow!

Canadian-born author Saul Bellow (1915–2005) considered Chicago his adopted city and, like Algren, many of his characters reside in the slummy streets of the city. He won the National Book Award three times, and the Nobel Prize for Literature in 1976, for "the human understanding and subtle analysis of contemporary culture that are combined in his work." His better-known novels include *Humboldt's Gift*, *Herzog* and *The Adventures of Augie March*. Bellow was not just a novelist, though; he was an acclaimed playwright and even played himself in Woody Allen's 1983 film *Zelig*.

A Staggering Genius

The writer Dave Eggers grew up in Lake Forest and attended the University of Illinois in Urbana-Champaign, where he received a degree in journalism. In 1998, he founded *McSweeneys*, a quarterly literary journal, and in 2000 he published *A Heartbreaking Work of Staggering Genius*, a wildly successful memoir about the death of his parents and the years he spent raising his younger brother after their parents' death. He also is the founder *The Believer*, a monthly magazine that he edits. Eggers' playful and experimental writing style—as well as his design sensibilities—has been a hit both critically and commercially, and he has gone on to write successful works of fiction, such as *You Shall Know Our Velocity* and *What is the What*.

Yet Another Genius

Acclaimed novelist and essayist David Foster Wallace (born February 21, 1962) spent his childhood in central Illinois, the son of a philosophy professor at the University of Illinois at Urbana-Champaign. Wallace himself later taught in the English department at Illinois State University in Normal during the 1990s. His debut novel, *The Broom of the System*, was published in 1987 and was well received, but his follow-up novel, the 1996 thousand-page behemoth *Infinite Jest*, is considered a masterpiece of modern fiction. Largely as a result of this success, in 1997, Wallace received the prestigious MacArthur Foundation "genius grant"—an annual award of $500,000 over five years, given to the brightest minds in America. His writing style is characterized by its sprawling and incredibly verbose prose, cultural and philosophical commentary and postmodern qualities.

ILLINOIS
INSIDER

Chicago poet Gwendolyn Brooks (1917–2000) won the Pulitzer Prize in 1950 for her book, *Annie Allen*. She was the first African American woman to ever receive the honor.

A True Chicago Stud

Louis "Studs" Terkel (born May 16, 1912) moved from New York to Chicago when he was a child and went on to become one of the great chroniclers of Chicago in the 20th century. He graduated from the University of Chicago law school in 1934 but decided to pursue a career in radio acting and, later, as a disc jockey. Terkel was heavily involved in the community of writers in Chicago in the 1930s and '40s, and was an especially big fan of Nelson Algren, whom he praises as "the city's greatest writer." Like Algren, Terkel was drawn to the dark underbelly of American cities. He became famous for writing oral histories, such as *Division Street: America* (a history of Chicago told by its residents) and *The Good War*, an oral history of World War II that won the Pulitzer Prize in 1985. Terkel likes to call himself "a guerilla journalist with a tape recorder."

Oh, and the nickname "Studs"? It was taken from a book, of course: Chicago author James T. Ferrell wrote a trilogy of novels in the 1930s about a young Irish man raised on the south side of Chicago. The character's name was Studs Lonigan.

FILM AND TELEVISION

Movie Madness

A number of movies have been filmed in Illinois. Here is a partial list:

A League of Their Own (1992)

About Last Night (1986)

Adventures in Babysitting (1987)

The Amityville Horror (2005)

The Babe (1992)

Backdraft (1991)

Barbershop (2002)

Barbershop 2: Back in Business (2004)

Batman Begins (2005)

The Blues Brothers (1980)

The Breakfast Club (1985)

The Break-Up (2006)

Chain Reaction (1996)

Child's Play (1988)

Christmas Vacation (1989)

Christmas with the Kranks (2004)

The Color of Money (1986)

Curly Sue (1991)

The Dark Knight (2008)

Dennis the Menace (1993)

Eight Men Out (1988)

Ferris Bueller's Day Off (1986)

Field of Dreams (1989)

The Fugitive (1993)

Hard Ball (2001)

The Harder They Fall (1956)

Harry and Tonto (1974)

High Fidelity (2000)

Home Alone (1990)

Hoop Dreams (1994)

How the West Was Won (1962)

I Want Someone to Eat Cheese With (2006)

The Ice Harvest (2005)

In the Heat of the Night (1967)

Julius Caesar (1950)

Kissing a Fool (1998)

Let's Go to Prison (2006)

Little Big League (1994)

Looking for Mr. Goodbar (1977)

Mad Dog and Glory (1993)

Major League (1989)

Meet the Parents (2000)

Message in a Bottle (1999)

Michael (1996)

My Best Friend's Wedding (1997)

My Big Fat Greek Wedding (2002)

My Bodyguard (1980)

National Lampoon's Vacation (1983)

The Negotiator (1998)

Never Been Kissed (1999)

North by Northwest (1959)

Novocaine (2001)

Opportunity Knocks (1990)

Payback (1999)

Pennies from Heaven (1981)

Prelude to a Kiss (1992)

Richie Rich (1994)

Risky Business (1983)

Road to Perdition (2002)

Rudy (1993)

Running Scared (1986)

Save the Last Dance (2001)

She's Having a Baby (1988)

Silver Streak (1976)

Sixteen Candles (1984)

Soul Food (1997)

The Sting (1973)

Stranger Than Fiction (2006)

Stuart Saves His Family (1995)

Touch and Go (1986)

Uncle Buck (1989)

The Untouchables (1987)

U.S. Marshalls (1998)

Wayne's World (1992)

Weird Science (1985)

What Women Want (2000)

When Harry Met Sally (1989)

While You Were Sleeping (1995)

Wicker Park (2004)

With Honors (1994)

The first movie ever filmed in Illinois was *The Tramp and the Dog*, made in 1896 by Chicago native William Nicholas Selig.

The Man Behind Mickey

Voice actor, animator, director, screenwriter, producer, theme park designer: in the world of entertainment, Walt Disney (1901–66) did it all. But before he moved to Hollywood and became one of the greatest successes of the 20th century, Disney was honing his skills at McKinley High School in Chicago, where he was a cartoonist for the school newspaper. He went on to write, direct and produce *Steamboat Willie*, the 1928 animated film featuring Mickey Mouse that was the first cartoon with sound to reach a wide audience. Over the years, creations such as Minnie Mouse, Pluto, Goofy and Donald Duck emerged from Disney's imagination to become some of the most famous and loved characters in the world. Today, The Walt Disney Company—which now includes theme parks, a Hollywood studio and television networks—lives on as one of the biggest and most influential (and certainly one of the most profitable) media and entertainment groups in the world.

DID YOU  KNOW?

Disney received more Academy Awards than any other individual in the history of the award, with 26 (four of which were honorary). He also has been nominated more than anyone else—a staggering 59 times!

The Queen of Talk

Although Oprah Winfrey is one of the most famous names associated with Chicago, she was actually born in Mississippi in 1954. She didn't move to Illinois until 1984, when she became the host of *AM Chicago*, a local talk show that soared to

number one within a month of Oprah's arrival. Within a year, the show expanded to one hour and was renamed *The Oprah Winfrey Show*. In 1986, Winfrey was nominated for an Academy Award for Best Supporting Actress for her role in *The Color Purple*. From that time on, it's been an absolute windfall: Oprah is considered by many to be the most influential woman in the world. She was the first woman to own and produce her own television show (which also happens to be the highest-rated talk show in television history). She publishes a magazine, *O, The Oprah Magazine* and hosts the most important (sales-wise, at least) book club in the entire world.

More Oprah

It's nearly impossible to overstate or exaggerate Oprah's cultural significance and influence. Some more details on this ultra-mega-worldwide superstar:

☛ Oprah's name was originally spelled "Orpah" on her birth certificate, but she changed the spelling because people found it difficult to pronounce.

☛ Oprah became pregnant at the age of 14, but the baby died shortly after birth as a result of complications.

☛ Oprah's production company is called Harpo Productions—"Harpo" is her name spelled backwards.

☛ 100 million people viewed Oprah's 1993 televised interview with Michael Jackson—the most-watched interview in TV history.

☛ In addition to *The Oprah Winfrey Show*, Harpo produces the daytime TV hits *Dr. Phil* and *The Rachael Ray Show*. Harpo also produced the 1998 film *Beloved*, based on the author Toni Morrison's Pulitzer Prize–winning novel of the same name.

☛ Oprah is a co-founder of the Oxygen Network, which launched in 2000.

☛ In 2001, Oprah purchased a 42-acre estate in Montecito, California. The price tag: a reported $50 million, making it one of the most expensive homes in the United States.

☛ During the taping of a show in late 2006, Oprah gave every member of her studio audience debit cards worth $1000—on the condition that they give the money to a charity of their choosing.

☛ Oprah's Book Club partners with the American Library Association (ALA) to distribute free copies of books donated by publishers to libraries nationwide.

The Worst TV Show Ever

That's what TV Guide called *The Jerry Springer Show* in a 2002 issue ranking the worst television programs of all time. The notorious daytime talk show—commonly known as the trashiest show in the trash TV genre—debuted in 1991 from the NBC Tower in downtown Chicago, where it still broadcasts today. Springer is a former mayor of Cincinnati who earned his law degree at Northwestern University, and it might surprise some to learn that the show has not always featured strippers, transvestites and, shall we say, kissing cousins. It began as a fairly conservative show, focusing on meat-and-potato political topics such as homelessness. However, in order to get ahead in the ratings, the show switched gears to the more sensational, circus-freak format that exists today.

And…it worked. For a while in the late 1990s, the show consistently beat Oprah in the ratings, reeling in 12 million viewers a day. Springer has used the show to continually court controversy throughout his career, most memorably with the episode, "I Married a Horse," in which a man came on the show and described his five-year marriage to a horse; and a woman regaled the audience with a story about her love affair with her dog. Many stations refused to air the episode, but the crowds obviously loved it. As for the critics of his show, Springer simply says, "It's just a show. It's not the end of Western civilization."

Siskel and Ebert and Roeper

Roger Ebert (born June 18, 1942) is the current host of *Ebert and Roeper*, the former host of *Siskel and Ebert*, a native of Urbana, and probably the most famous film critic in America. He got his start writing film reviews for the *Chicago Sun-Times* in 1967; at the time, he was a PhD candidate for English at the University of Chicago. In 1976, Ebert, and Gene Siskel, a film critic for the rival paper the *Chicago Tribune*, collaborated to host a television show for the local Chicago PBS station. The show was called *Sneak Previews*, and it's where the two men popularized their "Thumbs Up/Thumbs Down" rating system. Eventually the show moved from public broadcasting and became a nationally syndicated hit. Siskel died of complications from surgery to remove a brain tumor in 1999, and Richard Roeper of the *Sun-Times* was chosen as his permanent successor in 2000. That same year, the Film Center of the School of the Art Institute of Chicago was renamed the Gene Siskel Film Center. Siskel was a public fan and a loyal supporter of the center since its opening.

Sitcomapalooza

Illinois has been the setting for a number of successful television sitcoms over the years. Here are a few choice ones:

☞ *Perfect Strangers* starred Mark Linn-Baker and Bronson Pinchot as Larry and Balki, distant cousins who become roommates in Chicago. The slapstick comedy aired on ABC from 1986 until 1993, and in the early 1990s was a part of the network's TGIF lineup.

☞ *Married...with Children* aired from 1987 to 1997, lasting 11 seasons on FOX, where it was the first series the network aired. The Bundys—Al, Peg, Kelly and Bud—lived in Chicago.

☞ *Roseanne*, which aired from 1988 to 1997 and starred Roseanne Barr and John Goodman, was set in the fictional town of Lanford, Illinois. The show became famous for its realistic depiction of lower-income family life in Middle America, and it ranked in the top five in the Nielsen ratings during its first six seasons.

☞ Many don't know it, but the ABC sitcom *Family Matters* (another TGIF mainstay) was actually a spin-off of *Perfect Strangers*; the character Harriette Winslow, who lived in Larry and Balki's building, was given her own show in 1989. *Family Matters* focused on Harriette's life raising a family in Chicago and is most famous for the character of Steve Urkel, a nerdy next-door neighbor of the Winslows who popularized the catchphrase, "Did I do that?" The show is one of the most successful comedies in TV history to feature a largely African American cast. It aired from 1989 to 1998.

The Second City

The gold standard for improvisational comedy, The Second City theatre opened in Chicago in 1959. The comedy troupe has since spread to cities such as Toronto, Detroit, Los Angeles and Las Vegas, but the heart and soul of the institution continues on most significantly in Illinois. Many famous comedians and performers cut their teeth writing and performing skits at the Second City. It is now a full-fledged school with over 1400 students eager to learn improvisational comedy and comedy writing from some of the masters. Notable alumni of the Chicago troupe include:

John Belushi	Bonnie Hunt
Steve Carell	Shelley Long
Steven Colbert	Bill Murray
Chris Farley	Mike Myers
Tina Fey	Amy Sedaris

DID YOU KNOW?

It appears that Steven Colbert and Steve Carell just can't seem to get enough of each other. Colbert, now host of the popular Comedy Central fake news program *The Colbert Report*, began his career as an understudy for Steve Carell at Second City. The two Steves later collaborated on the short-lived *The Dana Carvey Show*, where they did the voices of Ace and Gary on the Ambiguously Gay Duo cartoon (which was later picked up and popularized by *Saturday Night Live*). Both got their big breaks, though, as correspondents for *The Daily Show*. And it's been nothing but success for both since.

Famous Stars Born in Illinois

☛ Joan Allen, *The Ice Storm*, *The Upside of Anger* (August 20, 1956, in Rochelle)

☛ Patricia Arquette, *True Romance*, *Medium* (April 8, 1968, in Chicago)

☛ Mary Astor, *The Maltese Falcon*, *Meet Me in St. Louis* (May 3, 1906, in Quincy)

☛ Dan Castellenaneta, voice of Homer Simpson (October 29, 1957, in Oak Park)

☛ John Cusack, *Say Anything*, *High Fidelity* (June 28, 1966, in Evanston)

☛ Buddy Ebsen, *The Beverly Hillbillies* (April 2, 1908, in Belleville)

☛ Jennie Garth, *Beverly Hills 90210*, *What I Like About You* (April 3, 1972, in Urbana)

☛ Kathy Griffin, *Suddenly Susan*, *Kathy Griffin: My Life on the D-List* (November 4, 1960, in Oak Park)

☛ Charlton Heston, *Ben-Hur*, *Planet of the Apes* (October 4, 1924, in Evanston)

☛ Rock Hudson, *Magnificent Obsession*, *Pillow Talk* (November 17, 1925, in Winnetka)

☛ John Malkovich, *Dangerous Liaisons*, *Of Mice and Men* (December 9, 1953, in Christopher)

☛ Bill Murray, *Saturday Night Live*, *Groundhog Day* (September 21, 1950, in Wilmette)

- Bob Newhart, *The Bob Newhart Show* (September 5, 1929, in Oak Park)

- Bob Odenkirk, *Mr. Show* (October 22, 1962, in Naperville)

- Jeremy Piven, *Entourage, Grosse Point Blank, PCU* (July 26, 1965, in Evanston)

- Richard Pryor, *See No Evil, Hear No Evil*; *Brewster's Millions* (December 1, 1940, in Peoria)

- Aidan Quinn, *Michael Collins, Bury My Heart at Wounded Knee* (March 8, 1959, in Rockford)

- Denise Richards, *Wild Things, The World is Not Enough* (February 17, 1971, in Downers Grove)

- Gary Sinise, *Forrest Gump, Apollo 13, CSI: New York* (March 17,1955, in Blue Island)

- Lili Taylor, *Six Feet Under, Factotum* (February 20, 1967, in Glencoe)

IF YOU BUILD IT...

Windy City Skyscrapers

Chicago is home to some of the finest and most modern architecture in the United States, and there's a good reason for that: much of the city's downtown had to be rebuilt after the Great Chicago Fire of 1871. Out of those ashes rose a phoenix of originality and progressive thinking about what buildings could become. Here's some quick facts about a few of the more famous Chi-town structures:

☛ The Sears Tower is the tallest building in the United States (and, some argue, the world—there is much discussion as to what extent the antennas on the top of it constitute its actual height). From the sidewalk to the top of its western antenna, the building measures 1730 feet. At 1136 feet, the Aon Center on Randolph Street is the third-tallest building in the U.S., and the John Hancock Center on Michigan Avenue (1127 feet, not counting its antennae) is the fourth-tallest building in the U.S.

☛ Berntrand Goldberg constructed Marina City (two side-by-side buildings on the north bank of the Chicago River that many say resemble corncobs) in 1964 as a reaction against "white flight," the mid-century phenomenon of middle-class white people fleeing inner cities for the comforts of the suburbs. As such, the buildings combined residential and commercial aesthetics into one, in a sense creating a city inside of a building. Restaurants, shopping, a theater, a bowling alley and an ice rink were all available within the confines of Marina City. The first 19 floors of the buildings (which are identically designed) house a parking garage, and all the apartments (floors 21 through 60) are pie-shaped, giving each apartment a large balcony. Today, the skating rink and movie theater are gone, but the House of Blues now resides at the base of the building. Marina City is also recently famous for having graced the cover of the Chicago band Wilco's critically acclaimed 2002 album, *Yankee Hotel Foxtrot.*

☛ At over 4 million square feet, the Merchandise Mart was the single largest building in the world when construction on it finished in 1930—it even has its own zip code! The concept behind the Mart was to consolidate the scattered wholesale trading in Chicago into one location. It was built by Marshall Field and Company and sold to Joseph Kennedy (father of John F. and Robert) in 1945 and was owned by the Kennedy clan until 1998.

☛ The Smurfit-Stone Building, perhaps better known as the Diamond Building, is one of the most identifiable sights of the Chicago skyline. (Anybody who's ever seen *Adventures in Babysitting* will recognize it immediately, as it's featured prominently in the film.) The roof slants up sharply into the sky, and the building is said to be an anti-phallic (read: vaginal) symbol.

Powerhouse Firm

Skidmore, Owings and Merrill (SOM) is an architecture firm (one of the largest in the United States) based in Chicago that has built and designed, among other Chicago landmarks, the Sears Tower, the John Hancock Center, Millennium Park and the soon-to-be-finished Trump International Hotel and Tower. SOM also won the coveted design contract for the Freedom Tower in New York City, which will be built in the spot where the World Trade Center used to stand.

The Grandaddy of Them All

Frank Lloyd Wright (1867–1959) is the most famous architect in American history, and he made his home in Oak Park, Illinois, for over 20 years. No state has more examples of Wright's work than Illinois—not even his home state of

Wisconsin. It is also where Wright developed his influential "prairie style" (fitting, as he was residing in the Prairie State), best represented by the Robie House in Chicago. Other famous Illinois Wright structures include the Unity Temple in Oak Park (he designed many houses in Oak Park), the Ward Willits House in Highland Park and the Dana-Thomas House in Springfield.

In 1914, while Wright was in Chicago overseeing work on a project called Midway Gardens, one of the servants at his Wisconsin estate (which Wright called Taliesin) set fire to the living quarters of the home and murdered seven people with an ax, including Mamah Borthwick, a woman with whom Wright had been having an open affair, and her two children.

SOME REAL CHARACTERS

The Robed One

Few men in the United States—indeed, perhaps the entire world—inspire more envy from males than Mr. Hugh Hefner, born April 9, 1926, in Chicago. The *Playboy* founder and editor-in-chief influenced American culture in a profound way during the last half of the 20th century, and he is often credited with helping to launch the sexual revolution. "Hef" was Chicago through and through—he was the reigning king of the city from the '50s through the early '70s, when he moved to California. But Chicago was where he made his name and also where he opened the first of his famous Playboy clubs. More about His Hefness and the nudie magazine that changed the world:

☞ Hef graduated from the University of Illinois at Urbana-Champaign in 1949, earning his psychology degree in less than three years.

☞ He also took classes at the Art Institute of Chicago (where he studied anatomy) and Northwestern University (where Hef took graduate courses in sociology and, as a sign of things to come, wrote a term paper on the subject of U.S. sex laws).

☞ After college, Hef was an aspiring cartoonist, and although he was unable to sell any of his ideas for a strip, he did publish a book of cartoons about Chicago, called *That Toddlin' Town*.

☞ Hef briefly worked as a copywriter for *Esquire* in Chicago but quit when he was denied a $5 raise.

☞ In order to finance the first issue of *Playboy*, Hefner took out loans from a number of people, including his mother, and used the furniture in his home as collateral for a bank loan.

☞ The first issue of *Playboy* hit newsstands in December 1953 and featured Marilyn Monroe on the cover.

☞ Hef selected a rabbit as the symbol of the magazine because he felt it was "an image that was frisky and playful...and the tuxedo added a sense of sophistication."

☞ Hef was arrested for obscenity in 1963 for *Playboy*'s pictorial of actress Jayne Mansfield. The trial ended in a hung jury.

☞ When Playboy Enterprises went public in 1971, the magazine was selling seven million copies a month throughout the world.

☞ An estimated 15 million people worldwide read *Playboy* every month.

☛ Playmates of the Month receive $25,000 from *Playboy*; the Playmate of the Year receives $140,000, a car and a motorbike.

☛ Hef has an IQ of 152, which qualifies him as a genius.

☛ Hef's three girlfriends—Bridget, Holly and Kendra—were the stars of the E! Series *The Girls Next Door*.

☛ Hef actually has a species named after him: *sylvilagus palustris hefneri*, which is an endangered species of marsh—wait for it—rabbits.

And on the Flip Side of the Coin...

Betty Friedan (1921–2006) was born in Peoria, and in 1963, she published one of the most influential books of the 20th century, *The Feminine Mystique*. At her 15-year reunion at Smith College, Friedan gave her fellow alumni a survey, asking the women to answer some questions about how they felt about their lives. The results confirmed what Friedan had for many years suspected: that many women in America were unhappy with their lives and did not know why. She wrote a magazine article on the subject, but three leading women's magazines at the time refused to publish it. So Friedan decided to expand it and write a book about what she considered the lost potential of women in modern American society. The book became a controversial bestseller and solidified her as the unofficial spokeswoman of the women's movement of the 1960s and '70s. Friedan also founded the U.S. National Organization for Women (NOW) in her apartment in 1966; today it has 500,000 members. As of 2000, *The Feminine Mystique* had sold three million copies worldwide.

America's Investigator

One of the most renowned investigative journalists in America comes from the Windy City: Seymour "Sy" Hersh was born there on April 8, 1937. Hersh was raised on the south side of the city and attended the University of Chicago. He made his name as a relentless reporter by breaking the story on the My Lai Massacre in Vietnam in 1969 (for which he won the 1970 Pulitzer Prize) and by reporting on the CIA for *The New York Times* in the 1970s. His controversial topics have included a scathing portrayal of John F. Kennedy's White House, Henry Kissinger's role in the Nixon White House and, most recently, the torture and abuse of detainees at Abu Ghraib prison.

LOOK, DON'T TOUCH!

Illinois is home to many world-class attractions.
Listed below are some of the more important ones.

Field Museum

The Field Museum of Natural History in Chicago is the most
popular cultural attraction in Chicago. It's named after famous
Illinois entrepreneur Marshall Field, who provided significant
funding during the museum's early years. The contents of the
Field Museum can be divided into four main sections: zoology,
anthropology, geology and botany. Especially popular exhibits
include Sue, the world's largest and most complete *Tyrannosaurus
rex* fossil; a large collection of Native American artifacts; and
Inside Ancient Egypt, complete with mummies and ancient
hieroglyphics.

Shedd Aquarium

The John G. Shedd Aquarium in downtown Chicago was the
world's largest indoor aquarium when it opened in 1930. It
holds five million gallons of water, over 22,000 animals and is
the second most popular cultural attraction in the city, receiving
two million visitors each year. In 1971, the aquarium added a
90,000-gallon tank that reproduced a Caribbean coral reef. Also
of note is Granddad, a Queensland lungfish brought to Shedd
in 1933. Amazingly, Granddad is still alive today and is considered the oldest captive fish in the world. The aquarium is also
environmentally conscious: in 2004, the roof was replaced with
a coating of 36 acres of liquefied soybeans in order to conserve
energy and cut down on pollution.

Art Institute of Chicago

The third most popular cultural attraction in Chicago, this art museum (founded in 1879) is home to some truly fine art. It is perhaps most famous for its impressionist, post-impressionist and modern American paintings. Included in the collection are *Nighthawks*, by Edward Hopper; *American Gothic*, by Grant Wood; *Bedroom in Arles*, by Vincent Van Gogh; and over 30 works by Claude Monet, as well as some from his *Water Lilies* series. The institute is also home to the School of the Art Institute of Chicago, one of the top graduate schools in the nation for fine arts. Painter Georgia O'Keeffe attended the school in 1905–06 but did not graduate. Other famous students at the school include authors Sarah Vowell (MA, 1996) and David Sedaris (BFA, 1987), and filmmaker Orson Welles.

Zoo's the Boss

The Lincoln Park Zoo in Chicago (founded in 1868) is the oldest, free public zoo in the United States, and from 1950 to 1955, the television show *Zoo Parade* was filmed on the grounds.

The Brookfield Zoo (opened in 1934 and located in the city's suburbs) is famous for being a largely "barless" zoo. No, that doesn't mean there's nowhere to have a cocktail (although certainly alcohol is not permitted); it means that Brookfield's designers used moats and other natural barriers as a way of separating the animals, instead of cages. It was also the first American zoo to feature a giant panda.

INVENTORS AND CREATORS

Genetic Genius

James D. Watson (born April 6, 1928, in Chicago) is best known for discovering, along with fellow biologist Francis Crick, the structure of the DNA molecule—widely considered one of the most significant scientific breakthroughs of the 20th century. He was awarded the Nobel Prize for physiology and medicine in 1962 and published *The Double Helix*, an account of his discoveries in genetics, in 1968. (The book ranked number seven on the Modern Library's list of the best non-fiction books of the 20th century.) In 1988, Watson was appointed as the Head of the Human Genome Project, though he resigned in 1992 amid conflict with his colleagues. Well before these great achievements, Watson enrolled at the University of Chicago at the tender age of 15, gaining his BSc in Zoology from the school in 1947.

A Pioneer of Silicon Valley

Arnold Orville Beckman (1900–2004) was born in Cullom, Illinois, and his scientific curiosity and prowess was evident from an early age: by the time he was 10 years old, he had constructed, with the help of his father, a chemistry laboratory in the tool shed in his family's backyard. He later attended the University of Illinois, where he received his bachelor's degree in chemical engineering in 1922 and a master's degree in physical chemistry in 1923. Beckman later moved to California, where in 1934 he invented the pH meter as a way of helping an old classmate figure out the acidity levels of lemon juice. This invention helped him start his own company, Beckman Instruments, which in 1955 hired William Shockley (co-inventor of the transistor) to be in charge of their new semiconductor operation in

Mountain View, California. Fifty years later, this area is the high-tech hub of the nation. At the time of his death—at 104 years old!—Beckman owned 14 patents and had donated, through his philanthropic foundation, over $300 million to science education programs and laboratories across the U.S.

Microsoft Man

Ray Ozzie was raised in Park Ridge, and attended the University of Illinois, where he graduated in 1979 with a degree in computer science. It would come in handy: Ozzie later created Lotus Notes, an influential messaging and groupware software from IBM. This success led him to Microsoft in 2005, at which time he became the chief technical officer of Microsoft, a job occupied previously by Bill Gates—pretty big shoes to fill!

A Sound Thinker

Over the course of his life, Marvin Camras (1916–95) was the recipient of over 500 patents. Perhaps most significantly, he invented the magnetic tape recording method used today for cassette and videotapes, floppy disks and credit card magnetic strips. Other inventions include multi-track recording, magnetic soundtracks for motion pictures, and the prototype of a video tape recorder. He's also Illinoisan through and through: he was born in Chicago and received his bachelor's degree, master's degree, and later was an instructor, at the Armour Institute of Technology (today the Illinois Institute of Technology).

DID YOU KNOW?

The first patent granted to an African American in Illinois was to Solomon McWorter of Barry, Illinois, on November 5, 1867. The patent was for "Improvement in Evaporators for Sorghum and Other Syrups."

A LED-er of the Scientific Community

Nick Holonyak was born in Zeigler on November 3, 1928, and is responsible for the creation of a very important electronic tool: the LED (light emitting diode), which he invented in 1962 while working at General Electric. These little babies are responsible for a number of things we take for granted in our accelerated technological world, such as forming the numbers on digital clocks, traffic lights, and the transmission of information from remote controls. LEDs are also starting to replace incandescent bulbs and fluorescent tubes around the world due to their longer life, energy efficiency and the wide range of colors they come in. The son of a coal miner, Holonyak received his undergraduate, master's degree and PhD from the University of Illinois at Urbana-Champaign.

Organ Donor

Laurens Hammond (1895–1973) was born in Evanston and became an engineer and, later, was the inventor of the Hammond organ. In his patent application, Hammond described his creation as an "electrical musical instrument" that recreated a sound similar to a pipe organ, which is a pretty accurate definition of the device. He intended the organ to be an affordable substitute for pianos for middle-class families, but the instrument was later utilized by jazz and rock musicians (Allman Brothers, Led Zeppelin) in the 1960s and '70s because of its unique tone. Over one million Hammond organs have been sold since 1934, when he received his first patent for the Model A.

Kombat Kreator

Born in Chicago on March 30, 1964, Ed Boon is the creator of the wildly popular video game *Mortal Kombat*. He graduated from the University of Illinois in 1986 with a bachelor's degree in math and computer science. Boon also does effects for pinball machines and was the voice of Scorpion in the *Mortal Kombat* films.

Telephone Tiff

Alexander Graham Bell invented the telephone, right? Well, that depends on whom you ask. In fact, a number of people from all over the world lay claim to this creation, but the one with perhaps the best case besides Bell is Elisha Gray, who developed a prototype of the telephone in 1876 in Highland Park, Illinois. It's kind of a sticky situation: Gray had been working on inventions of this type for years (in 1875 he had received a patent for the acoustic telegraph), and on February 14, 1876, he filed a caveat with the U.S. Patent Office, which is essentially an announcement of an invention one expects to soon patent. The description in the caveat is "for transmitting vocal sounds telegraphically." However, just hours before, and unbeknownst to graphically." However, just hours before, and unbeknownst to Gray, Bell had applied for a patent (not just a caveat) for a device that would perform the exact same function. A legal battle followed that resulted in Bell being awarded the patent and, ultimately, credit in the history books for fathering one of the great inventions of the modern era.

DID YOU  KNOW?

Abraham Lincoln is the only U.S. president to ever receive a patent. On May 22, 1849, he was issued a patent for "a device for buoying vessels over shoals"—U.S. Patent No. 6469. He created the model by whittling it out of wood. However, Honest Abe was apparently too busy with his political career, and the invention was never manufactured or marketed.

Poppin' Fresh!
Charles Cretors of Chicago invented the first popcorn machine in 1885. In 1893, he patented his process of popping the popcorn in oil. He introduced his popcorn wagon at Chicago's Columbian Exposition that same year to rave reviews. Cretors wasn't done, though: in 1900, he unveiled the Special, the first large horse-drawn popcorn wagon. It might not come as a surprise to learn that popcorn was voted the official Illinois State Snack Food in 2003.

Dippin' Dots!
Since being invented by Southern Illinois University Carbondale graduate Curt Jones in 1987, Dippin' Dots have been called "The Ice Cream of the Future"—or at least that's the marketing slogan they've chosen to go with. This peculiar ice cream is made, as the company's website quite simply states, by "using super-cold freezing methods to make little beads of ice cream." The result is a cup of tiny, tingly, crunchy, flavored beads that more or less taste like ice cream. The product can now be found all around the world, especially at theme parks and festivals, but also at various franchised store locations.

My Bologna Has Two Names

Yes, the famous hot dog brand Oscar Mayer made its name in Illinois—Chicago, to be specific. It didn't invent the hot dog or bologna per se, but the company did patent packaged sliced bacon in 1924. And few would argue that the famous Wienermobile is one of the greatest creations of the 20th century...

ILLINOIS INSIDER DeKalb resident Joseph Glidden (1813–1906) received the patent for barbed wire in 1874. Glidden used a coffee bean grinder to create the barbs. The invention changed life in the American West, allowing ranchers to tame and control their livestock.

Nobel Prize Winners Associated with Illinois

2000: Jack S. Kilby shared the Nobel Prize in Physics for assisting in the development and invention of the microchip. He's also credited with inventing the handheld calculator while working for Texas Instruments in 1967. He received a BSc from U of I in 1947.

1993: Phillip A. Sharp shared the Nobel Prize in Medicine and Physiology for his discovery of split genes. Sharp proved that genes are often composed of many different, separate segments. He received a PhD in chemistry from U of I in 1969.

1992: Edwin Krebs shared the Nobel Prize in Medicine and Physiology with Edmond Fischer for discoveries they made in the 1950s regarding how reversible protein phosphorylation can regulate a number of cellular processes. Krebs earned his BA from U of I in 1940.

1978: Hamilton Smith shared the Nobel Prize in Medicine and Physiology for "the discovery of restriction enzymes and their application to problems of molecular genetics." He spent much of his childhood in Urbana and attended U of I from 1948 to 1950.

1977: Rosalyn Sussman Yalow shared the Nobel Prize in Medicine and Physiology for her discovery of a technique that measures the levels of insulin and hormones in the blood and in body tissues. She was only the second woman to win the Nobel Prize in Medicine, and she received her master of science and her PhD from the U of I.

1972: John Robert Schrieffer shared the Nobel Prize in Physics with fellow U of I faculty members John Bardeen and Leon Cooper for their work on the theory of superconductivity. Schrieffer was born in Oak Park and received a Master of Science (1954) as well as a PhD (1957) from the university and served on the faculty until 1962.

1968: Luis Alvarez won the Nobel Prize in Physics for his work in researching particle accelerations. He was also a key partici-pant in the Manhattan Project during World War II. Alvarez received his bachelor's and master's degrees, as well as his PhD, from the University of Chicago.

1968: Robert Holley won the Nobel Prize in Medicine and Physiology for his work determining the precise structure of nucleic acids. He was born in Urbana and received his bachelor's degree from U of I in 1942.

1955: Vincent Du Vigneaud won the Nobel Prize in Chemistry for his work on "biochemically important sulfur compounds, especially for achieving the first synthesis of a polypeptide hormone." He was born in Chicago and earned both his bachelor's and master's degrees at U of I and also served on the faculty there from 1929 to 1932.

1955: Polykarp Kusch—a man whose name even *sounds* scientific—shared the Nobel Prize in Physics for his work in determining that the magnetic moment of the electron was greater than its theoretical value. He received a Master of Science and his PhD from U of I.

1952: Edward Purcell shared the Nobel Prize in Physics for his discovery of nuclear magnetic resonance in solids and liquids. He was born in Taylorville in 1912.

1946: Wendell Stanley shared the Nobel Prize in Chemistry for his contributions to the preparation of enzymes and virus proteins in pure form. He received a Master of Science and a PhD from U of I.

1943: Edward Doisy shared the Nobel Prize in Medicine and Physiology for discovering the chemical nature of vitamin K. He was born in Hume and received his Master of Science degree from the University of Illinois at Urbana-Champaign.

1937: Clinton Davisson shared the Nobel Prize in Physics for his discovery of electron diffraction. He was born in Bloomington and briefly attended the University of Chicago.

KEEPING THE PEACE

Inane Illinois Laws

Some of these crazy codes have been repealed, but some still exist as city ordinances, believe it or not.

☛ It's illegal in Cicero to hum on a public street on a Sunday.

☛ In Eureka, men with moustaches are not allowed to kiss women.

☛ Bowling is prohibited in Evanston.

☛ Don't even think about burning bird feathers while in Galesburg.

☛ Galesburg citizens will also be fined $1000 if they feel the need to beat rats with a baseball bat.

- In Homer, only the police are allowed to use slingshots.

- Mispronouncing "Joliet" while in the city limits will result in a $5 fine. (Just so you know, it's "Joe-lee-ette," not "Jaw-lee-ette.")

- No skating at Riverside Pond in Moline during June and August. (Apparently skating on the pond in July is okay, though.)

- In order to ward off the threat of gambling, pool tables are not allowed in the public establishments of Orland Park.

- No spitting on the sidewalk in Ottawa.

- In Peoria, it is illegal to put up a basketball hoop on a driveway.

- You can't make faces at a dog if you happen to find yourself in Normal—it's considered animal cruelty.

- Springfield bars strictly forbid the practice of "dwarf-tossing."

- From 1923 to 1969, the official language of Illinois was not English, but "American."

- Domesticated animals in Zion are forbidden from enjoying lit cigars.

And then, of course, there is Chicago, where…

- It's illegal to eat in a building that is on fire.

- Kites are not allowed within the city limits.

- You cannot fish while sitting on a giraffe's neck.

- Dogs are not allowed to drink whiskey.

The Biggest Mob Boss of All

The most notorious gangster in what at the time was the United States' most corrupt city, Al Capone (1899–1947) ran the Chicago underworld during the Prohibition years of the 1920s and 1930s. Originally from Brooklyn, Capone moved to the Windy City in 1919; by 1922, he had his hand in bootlegging, prostitution and gambling, and by 1925 he was in charge of the "Chicago Outfit," which was (and still is) the center of organized crime in the city. (The Bureau of Internal Revenue estimated that the Outfit took in $105 million in 1927 alone. On his business card, Capone claimed to be a used furniture dealer.)

"Scarface," as he was called, is perhaps most famous for the St. Valentine's Day Massacre, in which four of Capone's men dressed up as police officers and brutally gunned down six members of a rival gang (and one unlucky optometrist) in a warehouse on Valentine's Day of 1929. No one was ever charged with the murders, although it was common knowledge that Capone was the man behind it all. Authorities finally indicted him on income tax evasion charges in 1931, and he served seven years behind bars, much of it in Alcatraz. Released in 1939, he spent the remainder of his days in Florida, where his body and mind deteriorated from the effects of syphilis.

Killer Clown

One of the most infamous serial killers in American history, John Wayne Gacy (1942–94) was charged and convicted with the murder of 33 young men between 1972 and 1978. Gacy was born in Chicago, but also lived in the Illinois towns of Springfield and Des Plaines. He was finally caught when police, investigating the disappearance of a boy who had vanished on his way to a job interview with Gacy, came to his Des Plaines home to question him. He asked the officers to come in for coffee, at which point they detected a foul odor coming from the house, which they recognized as being the possible smell of decaying bodies. They subsequently obtained a search warrant to search his residence and found 29 bodies in a crawl space underneath the house. He later confessed to four more killings, saying he dumped their bodies in a river nearby. Gacy, himself a closeted homosexual, targeted homosexual young adult males, often by hiring them to work for his painting and maintenance company. At different points in his life, Gacy was a shoe salesman, a restaurant manager, a building contractor, and—terrifyingly—a children's clown (he called himself Pogo the Clown). He was sentenced to death in 1980 and executed by lethal injection in 1994.

DID YOU KNOW?

While on death row, Gacy discovered his inner artist and began oil painting as a hobby. His subject matter included figures such as Jesus, Elvis Presley and Mickey Mouse, and he had a particular interest in painting clowns, who had names such as Patches, Skull and Death, and, of course, Pogo. After his execution, many of these paintings were sold. One, which depicted dwarfs playing baseball against the Chicago Cubs, fetched $9500 at an auction. Perhaps unsurprisingly, not everyone was so eager to hang a serial killer's pictures on their walls: a bonfire was organized in June 1994 in Naperville, where over 300 people watched 25 of Gacy's paintings burn.

Thrill Killers

Nathan Leopold Jr. (born November 19, 1904) and Richard Loeb (born June 11, 1905) were graduate students at the University of Chicago in 1924 when they murdered 14-year-old Bobby Franks, a neighbor of Loeb. Leopold and Loeb had no motive for the murder other than wanting to prove to themselves that they were intelligent enough to commit the perfect crime. Needless to say, things didn't go according to plan. Hauled in for questioning after the typewriter used for the ransom note was traced back to Leopold, both men's alibis broke down and each confessed to the murder. They were eventually sentenced to life in prison, plus 99 years. More details about this disturbing crime:

☛ Both men were well educated—Loeb was the youngest undergrad in the history of the University of Michigan at 17 years of age.

☛ Clarence Darrow—later famous for defending John T. Scopes in the 1925 "Scopes-Monkey" trial—was the defense attorney for Leopold and Loeb at their trial.

A longtime opponent of capital punishment, Darrow had the two killers plead guilty to the murder in the hopes that their admission of guilt would convince the judge to spare them the death penalty.

☛ In front of Judge John Caverly of Cook County, Darrow made a now-legendary 12-hour summation speech in which he argued that, among other things, it was unfair to hang two young men who were emotionally immature and sexually confused, and who had obsessively misinterpreted the teachings of Friedrich Nietzsche that they had learned while at university.

☛ In 1936, a fellow inmate at Joliet Prison attacked Loeb with a razor blade in the showers; Loeb subsequently died from the wounds.

☛ Leopold allegedly had an IQ of 210 and spoke 15 languages.

☛ In 1958, Leopold was released after 33 years in prison. He moved to Puerto Rico, where he received a master's degree, and taught mathematics.

☛ After his release, Leopold wrote an autobiography entitled *Life Plus 99 Years*. In it, he stated that if asked to name the two men who "came closest to preaching the pure essence of love," he would have responded that it was Jesus and Clarence Darrow.

☛ The crime inspired a 1929 play called *Rope*, which Alfred Hitchcock later made into a film in 1948.

Not a Speck of Morality

On July 13, 1966, Richard Speck (born December 6, 1941, in Kirkwood) broke into a townhouse on the south side of Chicago, the home of several student nurses who worked at the nearby South Chicago Community Hospital. He took nine nurses hostage and raped and killed eight of them over the course of the next few hours. Only one—Corazon Amurao—survived by hiding underneath a bed. In 1967, Speck was sentenced to death after only 49 minutes of jury deliberation; however, because it was later found that potential jurors were discriminated against based on their aversion to the death penalty, the death sentence was dropped. In 1972, Speck was re-sentenced to what could be interpreted as 1200 years in prison—eight consecutive sentences of 50 to 150 years. He died of a heart attack at Stateville Prison in Joliet on December 5, 1991, at the age of 49.

Foie Gras Controversy

In 2006, the Chicago City Council voted to ban the sale of foie gras in restaurants across the city. (For the uninitiated, foie gras, which literally means "fatty liver" in French, is a delicacy prepared by pumping the liver of a duck or goose with corn mush for a couple of weeks before it is slaughtered, thereby enhancing the taste.) Animal rights groups object to this process as being cruel to animals, while producers of foie gras contend that the process is not uncomfortable for the birds. Mayor Daley referred to the law as "the silliest law" the City Council had ever passed. Indeed, few in the city seem to take the ordinance seriously—warnings have been issued instead of fines, and the first restaurant owner to be written up (Doug Sohn of Hot Doug's) received only a paltry $250 fine for his foie gras "haute" dog.

A Potpourri of Illinois Crime Data

Like every state, Illinois struggles with crime. Here's a look at the state's crime statistics:

☛ In 2006, Illinois police reported 467,372 violent and property crimes, a 1.7 percent drop from the previous year.

☛ There were 766 murders in Illinois in 2005, part of a downward trend in state murders over the past decade.

☞ Murders went up in 2006, though, for the first time in five years.

☞ There were 467 murders in Chicago in 2006, up from 450 in 2005.

☞ As of January 1, 2007, Illinois had 11 prisoners on death row—25th out of the 38 states where the death penalty is still legal.

☞ The state of Illinois has put 12 people to death since 1976.

☞ You are 10 times more likely to get a death sentence in DuPage County than if you cross the border into Cook County.

☞ Illinois comes in fourth in most robberies per capita: 1.765 people per 1000 have been the victim of a robbery.

☞ There were 40,355 motor vehicle thefts in Illinois in 2004—10th highest in the nation.

Nine Illinois citizens lost their lives in the terrorist attacks of September 11, 2001.

Jailhouse Blues

Some little-known facts about the prisons and prisoners of Illinois…

☞ Stateville Correctional Center, a maximum-security prison in Crest Hill, Illinois, is home to the last remaining panopticon, or "roundhouse," in a U.S. prison. A panopticon is a design concept in which guards are placed in an armed tower in the center of the prison and are able to observe prisoners without prisoners knowing whether they are being observed. Stateville is also known for a controversy involving the use of prisoners as subjects for a study of possible malaria vaccines during World War II.

☛ On February 11, 1990, six "extremely dangerous" prisoners, including three convicted murderers, escaped Joliet Correctional Facility—a maximum-security prison—by sawing through their cell bars and squeezing out a window. All six were found within a month.

☛ Since it closed in 2002, Joliet Prison (which opened all the way back in 1858) has been no stranger to the world of entertainment. The first season of the FOX show *Prison Break* was shot there, as were the films *Derailed* (starring Clive Owen and Jennifer Aniston) and *Let's Go to Prison* (starring Dax Shepard and Will Arnett). Also, the Bob Dylan tune "Percy's Song" is about a man trying to get a friend's 99-year sentence at Joliet Prison repealed.

☛ Menard Correctional Center in Chester is the state's largest maximum-security prison and the second-oldest prison in the state. As of 2006, the population of inmates was an average of 3315. (In)famous inmates throughout the years have included John Wayne Gacy, Kenneth Allen, and Homer Van Meter, an associate of famed killer John Dillinger.

Don't Drive Drunk!

Here's the skinny on those unfortunate souls who drive under the influence (DUI) in Illinois:

☛ Illinois drunk drivers tend to be overwhelmingly male (84 percent!).

☛ The legal blood alcohol content (BAC) level limit in Illinois is 0.08.

☛ In 2005, 35 percent of all fatal car accidents in Illinois involved a BAC of 0.08 or higher.

- There were 580 alcohol-related traffic fatalities in 2005—eighth highest in the United States.

- First and second DUI offenses are class A misdemeanors; all subsequent offenses are considered class 4 felonies.

A COMPETITIVE EDGE

Illinois is home to teams in all four major North American sports—football, hockey, baseball and basketball—and all play their games in Chicago. The city is one of the best places in the world for a sports fan. However, be prepared to endure years of misery between championship titles. Especially if you're a baseball fan.

Crosstown Rivals

Chicago is home to two professional baseball teams—the Cubs and the White Sox—and both are said to have been burdened by curses from the baseball gods. The Cubs have only won the World Series twice, once in 1907 and again in 1908 (and since 1945 have not made the series), but the White Sox finally won the big game against the Houston Astros in 2005, breaking the 88-year "Black Sox" curse.

The Black Sox Scandal

The 1919 World Series pitted the Chicago White Sox against the Cincinnati Reds in a best-of-nine series (one of only four championship series in the history of the game that used this format as opposed to the traditional best-of-seven). However, the series was not legitimate: many members of the White Sox plotted along with gamblers to "throw" the series—that is, to lose on purpose. The Reds won the series in eight games, and after an investigation in 1920, eight players for the White Sox were permanently banned from the game. The most famous of these players, "Shoeless" Joe Jackson, still holds the record for best White Sox batting average of all time. Jackson's involvement in the controversy is disputed, mostly because his stats for the series are so strong (he batted .375 with 12 hits), and he

maintained his innocence even after being expelled from Major League Baseball. His last words are rumored to be, "I'm going to meet the greatest umpire of all now, and I know he will judge me innocent."

DID YOU  **KNOW?**

Shoeless Joe got his nickname in the minor leagues while playing a doubleheader. During the afternoon game, he wore a new pair of cleats that gave him blisters. So in the night game, he took his shoes off and played only in his socks. After he hit a triple and slid into third base, an angry fan of the opposing team yelled out, "Can't we stop this shoeless son-of-a-gun?"

The Curse of the Billy Goat

In the 1945 World Series, the Cubs were matched up against the Detroit Tigers, and they entered game four up two games to one. The day of the game, William "Billy Goat" Sianis, owner of the Billy Goat Tavern, showed up at the gates at Wrigley Field with two tickets: one for him and one for his pet goat, Murphy. He was denied entry and was told that no animals were allowed in the park. Sianis then appealed to Cubs owner Philip K. Wrigley, who said that he would let Billy in, but not the goat. When Sianis asked why the goat wasn't allowed, Wrigley said, "Because the goat stinks." Angered, Sianis threw up his arms and proclaimed, "The Cubs ain't gonna win no more. The Cubs will never win a World Series so long as the goat is not allowed in Wrigley Field." The Cubs lost the game, and the series, and "Billy Goat" sent a telegram to Wrigley asking, "Who stinks now?" The curse had begun, and they haven't reached the World Series since.

The Infamous Bartman

Here comes a sad one: In 2003, the Cubs faced the Florida Marlins in the National League Championship Series. They entered game six up three games to two, and by the eighth inning, they were leading 3–0 and only five outs away from reaching their first World Series in 58 years. But then disaster struck. Marlins batter Luis Castillo hit a pop fly towards left field that was headed foul towards the seats. A now-infamous man named Steve Bartman happened to be sitting where the ball was headed that night, and he reached out his hand to catch it. Unfortunately, he didn't realize that Cubs left fielder Moises Alou was trying to do the same thing, and Bartman ended up interfering with Alou's chance of catching the ball and putting the batter out.

During any other game, it would have been a relatively harmless mistake, but Bartman and the Cubs were out of luck that night. Following the incident, Castillo drew a walk, and the Marlins proceeded to score eight runs in that same inning, winning the game 8–3. Even worse, the next night the Marlins won again and advanced to the World Series, where they ended up beating the Yankees. Bartman, who was ushered out of Wrigley by stadium security that night, became the city's scapegoat and a modern symbol of the Cubbies' unshakable curse. Long-time Cubs fan Governor Blagojevich even chimed in, saying, "If [Bartman] ever commits a crime, he won't get a pardon from this governor." All for just for trying to catch a foul ball. Poor guy.

The Friendly Confines

The second-oldest professional ballpark in the country, Wrigley Field was constructed in 1914 and has been the home of the Cubs ever since. The stadium was originally known as Weeghman Park, after Charlie Weeghman who built it. In 1920, the Wrigley family bought it; it was known as Cubs Park until 1926, when it was named Wrigley Field in honor of William Wrigley Jr. The stadium was…

☛ The first ballpark to play organ music

☛ The first ballpark to let fans keep home-run balls

☛ The first ballpark with permanent concession stands

☛ The last ballpark to play a game at night, under the lights—which it didn't do until 1988! Before that the Cubbies only played day games while at home.

Also, if a ball gets stuck in the famous vines on the outfield wall of the field, it's an automatic double.

Holy Cow!
Chicago was the home of one of the most famous broadcasters to ever speak into the microphone, Harry Caray (1914–98).

The man is synonymous with Chicago Cubs baseball, and his one-of-a-kind renditions of "Take Me Out to the Ball Game" during the seventh-inning stretch will forever be a part of baseball legend. But what many outside of Chicago don't know is that he also worked in broadcasting for the Chicago White Sox for 11 seasons, from 1971 to 1981. Even more, he started his career doing games for the St. Louis Cardinals—the Cubbies' biggest rival—from 1945 to 1969. (He was born in St. Louis.) And before that, he had done football play-by-play for the University of Missouri, the alma mater of a certain author of this book. But in the end, Caray and his trademark oversized black glasses are etched into the public consciousness as a part of the Cubs, because it's where he became a national favorite (WGN's TV broadcast reached the entire U.S.). Caray was a quotable guy—here's a sample of his witticisms and catch-phrases:

☛ "It could be, it might be, it is! A home run!"

☛ "I always sing 'Take Me Out to the Ball Game' because it's the only song I know all the words to."

☛ "I've been [broadcasting] for 54 years now; with a little experience, I might get better."

☛ "Holy cow!"

☛ "I knew the profanity used up and down my street would not go over on the air, so I trained myself to say 'Holy cow' instead."

☛ "Now, you tell me, if I have a day off during the baseball season, where do you think I'll spend it? The ballpark. I still love it. Always have, always will."

DID YOU KNOW?

In 1906, the White Sox defeated the heavily favored Cubs in the World Series—the only time the two teams have met in a championship series.

There's No Crying in Baseball!

In 1943, with World War II raging across the Atlantic, Chicago Cubs owner Philip K. Wrigley founded the All-American Girls Professional Baseball League. It was an attempt to sustain the popularity of baseball while many of its professional players were serving overseas. Tryouts for the league were held at Wrigley Field, and many of the teams in the league hailed from Illinois towns, such as the Racine Belles, the Peoria Redwings, the Chicago Colleens and the Springfield Sallies. Femininity was valued by league ownership: the women were required to wear skirts and lipstick on the field, and to take etiquette classes. The league, largely forgotten, was commemorated (albeit fictionally) in the popular 1992 film *A League of Their Own*, which starred Geena Davis, Lori Petty, Rosie O'Donnell and Madonna.

DA BULLS

His Airness

Arguably the most famous name associated with Chicago—
though Oprah gives him a run for his money—Michael Jordan
dominated American basketball in the 1990s, winning six
championships in eight seasons for the Windy City's beloved
Bulls. He is considered by many to be the greatest player in the
history of the game, and for good reason—check out these stats
and records:

- Five MVP awards

- Fourteen All-Star appearances

- Ten scoring titles

- All-time highest career scoring average (30.1 points per game)

- Second-most steals in the history of the NBA (2514)

- Played on two Olympic gold medal–winning teams

- Most points in NBA playoff history (5987)

- Has appeared on the cover of *Sports Illustrated* a record *49* times!

It is impossible to overstate Michael Jordan's legacy to the sport of basketball, but he also changed the way in which athletes are marketed to the public—Jordan was (and still is) one of the most recognizable faces in the world because of his many endorsement deals with such brands as Gatorade, Hanes, Wheaties, McDonald's, Coca-Cola and, of course, Nike.

DID YOU KNOW?

After winning his third straight NBA championship in 1993, Jordan retired from the game to pursue a dream of playing professional baseball. It was not meant to be: he averaged an unimpressive .202 batting average for the Birmingham Barons, a minor-league farm team for the Chicago White Sox. (He also hit three home runs.) In 1995, he abandoned the idea and returned to playing for the Bulls, where he led his team to championships in '96, '97 and '98. During the 1995–96 season, Jordan's first year back, the Bulls lost only 10 games, posting a record of 72–10. It remains to this day the best single season record in the history of the NBA.

MORE SPORTS TIDBITS

Bears Team History

☛ The organization that would eventually become known as the Chicago Bears was originally the Decatur Staleys, named after the founder of the franchise, A.E. Staley. In 1921, the team moved to Chicago and became the Chicago Staleys. It wasn't until 1922 that the name was changed to the Chicago Bears. Staley's legacy is not entirely absent, though: since 2003, the official mascot of the team has been "Staley Da Bear."

☛ The Bears have the most players voted into the Pro Football Hall of Fame, at 26 inductees.

☛ In 1984, Bears running back Walter Payton broke Jim Brown's record for career rushing yards. He held the record until 2002, when Emmitt Smith surpassed him.

☛ The Bears have won nine NFL championships, but only one since 1970, when the NFL merged with the AFL. They won Super Bowl XX in 1985, with a team many analysts and experts consider the best in the history of the NFL (featuring the stars Payton, Mike Singletary and quarterback Jim McMahon).

☛ The 1985 team was nominated for a Grammy for the "The Super Bowl Shuffle," a humorous song the team recorded before the playoffs of that season. It reached number 41 on the Billboard pop charts. YouTube it.

☛ Former Bears lineman William "Refrigerator" Perry weighed 326 pounds and has the distinction of owning the largest Super Bowl ring of any player to have ever participated in the history of the game. Perry wears a size 25, whereas the average adult male wears between a 9 and 11.

☛ In 2006, Bears kick returner Devin Hester became the first player to return the opening kickoff of a Super Bowl for a touchdown. Unfortunately, the Bears lost to the Indianapolis Colts, 29–17.

Rudy! Rudy! Rudy!

Daniel Eugene "Rudy" Ruettiger (born August 23, 1948) was the inspiration for the 1993 film *Rudy*, one of the most popular sports movies of all time. Born in Joliet, he attended and played football for Joliet Catholic High School. Rudy was one of 14 children and dreamed of playing football for Notre Dame, but he was only 5 feet 6 inches and 165 pounds. He attended Holy Cross Junior College in South Bend, Indiana, and was rejected admission as a transfer student three times before finally being accepted to Notre Dame. We won't ruin the ending for you, but suffice it to say it's a pretty inspiring tale. Today Rudy writes books and is a motivational speaker, and it'll cost you roughly $17,500 to have him appear at your next corporate outing. Kinda steep!

 The Chicago Blackhawks were one of the six original teams in the National Hockey League—their franchise was founded in 1926. However, they've won only three Stanley Cups in their history, and their last title was almost 50 years ago, all the way back in 1961!

The New Boss

Bruce Weber (born October 19, 1956) is making a name for himself in Illinois athletics. As the head coach of men's basketball at Southern Illinois University from 1998 to 2003, he led the Salukis to the top of the Missouri Valley Conference and a somewhat unprecedented Sweet Sixteen appearance in the 2002 NCAA tournament. The following year, Weber was chosen to replace Bill Self as the head coach of the University of Illinois. In 2005, Weber took the Illini to the NCAA championship and, despite a loss, was awarded the Naismith College Coach of the Year and the Associated Press National Coach of the Year. As of 2007, Weber's record as coach of Illinois was 112–28, making the team tied for the most wins of any NCAA team over the course of the previous four seasons.

Quite a Catch

In 2005, Tim Pruitt of Godfrey was casually fishing in the Mississippi River near Alton and ended up catching a blue cat-fish that weighed 124 pounds, breaking the previous world record. The beast was 58 inches long and 44 inches around, and Pruitt fought with the fish for a full 30 minutes before finally reeling it in. The fish was so strong that it actually dragged Pruitt and his fellow fishing companions half a mile down the river. But the story has a sad ending. While being transported to be put on display in a tank in Kansas, the fish died.

The Need for Speed

In 2001, the Chicagoland Speedway, located just outside Joliet, held its first races. The racetrack, which can hold a crowd of 75,000, hosts the Busch Series and the Sprint Cup Series, as well as the Indy Racing League (IRL). Jimmie Johnson was the first driver to win a NASCAR event at the speedway, winning the Busch Series on July 14, 2001.

Athletic Figures Born In Illinois

☞ Dick Butkus (born December 9, 1946, in Chicago) is a true Illinoisan. He was a two-time All-American linebacker and center for the University of Illinois, and as a pro played for the Chicago Bears, where he was selected to the Pro Bowl eight times. He was inducted to the College Football Hall of Fame in 1983 and the Pro Football Hall of Fame in 1979. Known for his brutally punishing tackles, Butkus once appeared on the cover of *Sports Illustrated* with the caption, "The Most Feared Man in the Game."

☞ Jimmy Connors (born 1952, in East St. Louis). The left-handed tennis ace holds the record for most professional singles titles (109), most U.S. Open wins (98) and most Wimbledon wins (84). He's currently coaching American tennis phenom Andy Roddick.

☞ Kevin Duckworth (born April 1, 1964, in Harvey) was quite the physical specimen. Standing 7 feet tall and weighing in at about 275 pounds, "the Duck" played for a number of NBA teams, including the Milwaukee Bucks and the Washington Bullets, but most notably the Portland Trail Blazers, for whom he was a two-time All-Star (and also received the league's Most Improved Player award in 1987–88). Before all that, he was the center for Eastern Illinois University, in Charleston.

☞ Whitey Herzog (born November 9, 1931, in New Athens) managed the Texas Rangers, the California Angels, the Kansas City Royals, and the St. Louis Cardinals, for whom he won the World Series in 1982.

☞ Jackie Joyner-Kersee (born March 3, 1962, in East St. Louis) is considered one of the greatest female athletes in history. Joyner-Kersee was a four-year starter on the UCLA women's basketball team, and in 1998, UCLA honored her as one of the 15 best players in UCLA women's basketball. But Jackie is most famous for her prowess as a U.S. Olympian—she won six medals (two bronze, one silver and three gold) in the heptathlon and the long jump during her illustrious Olympic career.

☞ Mike Krzyzewski (born February 13, 1947, in Chicago) has been the head coach of Duke University since 1980. He has the most wins in the history of the NCAA tournament and has won three championship titles for the Blue Devils. In 2001, *Time* magazine named Krzyzewski "America's Best Coach."

☞ Mike Shanahan (born August 24, 1952, in Oak Park) attended Eastern Illinois University, where he was the football team's quarterback until he ruptured one of his kidneys during a practice, ending his playing career. He began coaching after graduating college, and in 1978 returned to EIU as the offensive coordinator, helping the team to a Division II title. Today, Shanahan is famous as the coach of the mighty Denver Broncos, whom he led to consecutive Super Bowl championships in 1998 and 1999.

☞ Lorezo Smith III (born February 27, 1978, in Kankakee) was a member of the four-man U.S. Olympic bobsled team during the 2006 games in Torino, Italy. Smith was also a captain in the U.S. Army and a member of both the army football team and track and field (his 4 x 100 meter relay team still holds the Academy record). A true American.

☛ Dwyane Wade (born January 17, 1982, in Chicago) was named the 2006 Sportsman of the Year by *Sports Illustrated* after his team, the Miami Heat, won the NBA championship. Wade receives frequent comparisons to Michael Jordan, whom he says he patterns his game after.

☛ Robin Yount (born September 16, 1955, in Danville) was a shortstop and center fielder who played every season from 1974 to 1993 with the Milwaukee Brewers. He's got quite a baseball résumé. Yount was elected to the Hall of Fame in 1999; he's one of only 27 players in the history of the game to collect over 3000 hits in his career. He had three All-Star selections, two Most Valuable Player Awards, and one Gold Glove, plus he holds the Brewers career records for, ahem, hits, doubles, triples, home runs, RBIs, walks, at-bats, games played and probably any other statistic you can dream of. Sure, the Brewers have never been very good, but those are still some impressive numbers.

TOP TEN REASONS TO LIVE IN ILLINOIS

10. You could always use a laugh, and some of the funniest people in the world gather together to put on skits every night at the Second City comedy theater in Chicago. Not to mention, Bill Murray grew up here.

9. You can pretend you're Huckleberry Finn in one of many Mississippi River towns located along the western border of the state. And if you're feeling adventurous, feel free to float down the river in a raft. But…be careful.

8. You get an extra day off work and school every year in honor of some guy named Casimir Pulaski who nobody outside of Illinois has ever heard of. (He was a former Polish politician who served as a general in the American Revolutionary War.)

7. Indulge your inner poet and walk in the footsteps of some of the greatest authors in American history—heavyweights such as Ernest Hemingway, Saul Bellow, Nelson Algren, Carl Sandburg and Gwendolynn Brooks.

6. As the home of McDonald's, Dairy Queen, Deep Dish pizza, and the Chicago Dog—not to mention miles and miles of corn—the Prairie State's a place where you'll never go hungry.

5. Three words: no more smoking. As of January 2008, state law requires smokers in bars and restaurants to take it outside. So you won't have to dry clean your clothes after a night out.

4. Feel presidential. Three U.S. presidents—Ulysses S. Grant, Ronald Reagan and Abraham Lincoln—have called Illinois

home. Which is not to even mention presidential hopefuls Hillary Clinton and Barack Obama.

3. The river's green! Every St. Paddy's Day, the Chicago River is dyed green in honor of every person with Irish ancestry in the city.

2. Sports addicts can go hog wild, rooting for teams renowned for success (the Bulls) and notorious for failure (the Cubs).

And the number one reason to spend some time in Illinois...

1. The winters are freezing, and the summers are blazing—but spring and fall make it all worth it.

ABOUT THE AUTHORS

David Hudnall

David Hudnall worked as a culture writer for an alternative weekly magazine before moving to Chicago to enter the MA in writing program at DePaul University. He has traveled the highways of the Midwest his whole life, both on business and on family road trips sitting alongside his two little sisters. He has discovered Midwesterners are hardly boring and far more down-to-earth than "those coastal types." In the future, David sees himself in media or publishing. He basically plans on riding out this whole writing thing until he can no longer afford to eat.

Lisa Wojna

Lisa is the co-author of at least 12 trivia books, as well as being the sole author of five other non-fiction books. She has worked in the community newspaper industry as a writer and journalist and has traveled all over the world. Although writing and photography have been a central part of her life for as long as she can remember, it's the people behind every story that are her motivation and give her the most fulfilment.

ABOUT THE ILLUSTRATORS

Peter Tyler

Peter is a recent graduate of the Vancouver Film School's Visual Art and Design and Classical animation programs. Though his ultimate passion is in filmmaking, he is also intent on developing his draftsmanship and storytelling, with the aim of using those skills in future filmic misadventures.

Roger Garcia

Roger Garcia was born in El Salvador and came with his parents to North America at the age of seven. Because of the language barrier, he had to find a way to communicate with other kids. That's when he discovered the art of tracing. It wasn't long before he mastered this highly skilled technique. He taught himself to paint and sculpt, and then in high school and college, Roger skipped class to hide in the art room all day in order to further explore his talent. Roger's work can be seen in many other Blue Bike trivia books.

Patrick Hénaff

Born in France, Patrick Hénaff is mostly self-taught. He is a versatile artist who has explored a variety of media under many different influences. He now uses primarily pen and ink to draw and then processes the images on computer. He is particularly interested in the narrative power of pictures and tries to use them as a way to tell stories.

Pat Bidwell

Pat has always had a passion for drawing and art. Initially self-taught, he completed art studies in Visual Communication in 1986. Over the years, he has worked both locally and internationally as an illustrator product designer and graphic designer, collecting many awards for excellence along the way. When not at the drawing board, Pat pursues other interests solo and or with his wife, Lisa, such as landscaping, gardening, traveling, the symphony and the opera.